GW00542477

CAMPING
guide to
TASMANIA

Craig Lewis and Cathy Savage

BOILING BILLY
PUBLICATIONS

www.boilingbilly.net.au

Boiling Billy
An imprint under license to
Woodslane Press Pty Ltd
10 Apollo Street
Warriewood NSW 2102 Australia
Email: info@woodslane.com.au
Tel: 02 8445 2300 Fax: 02 9997 5850
www.woodslane.com.au

This updated 4th edition 2013
Copyright © text Craig Lewis and Cathy Savage 2013
Copyright © photographs Craig Lewis/Boiling Billy Images 2013
ISBN: 9781922131317

Design and Layout: Erica McIntyre
Cartography: Tony Fakira

National Library of Australia Cataloguing-in-Publication entry
Author: Lewis, Craig (Craig William), 1966-
Title: Camping guide to Tasmania : the bestselling
              colour guide to over 150 campsites / Craig Lewis,
              Cathy Savage.
ISBN: 9781922131317 (pbk.)
Notes: Includes index.
Subjects: Camping--Tasmania--Guidebooks.
              Camp sites, facilities, etc.--Tasmania--Directories.
              National parks and reserves--Tasmania--Directories.
              Northern Territory--Guidebooks.
Other Authors/Contributors: Savage, Cathy.
Dewey Number: 919.46

Your Help Please

Boiling Billy Publications welcomes feedback from readers. If you find things are different than what is stated in this guide, or you know of a suitable campsite that we can update in subsequent editions, then please write or e-mail us at

Boiling Billy Publications
Nimmitabel NSW 2631
Tel: 02 6454 6162
E-mail: info@boilingbilly.com.au
Web: www.boilingbilly.net.au
www.facebook.com/boilingbilly

follow us on

ABOUT the authors

Craig Lewis and Cathy Savage have travelled extensively throughout Australia over the last 17 or so years, visiting some of the very best camping destinations secreted away across this vast country.

The pair reckon that the wide open spaces of the Australian outdoors is a great place to be, so after intermittent stints of travelling between work commitments, they began submitting magazine and newspaper travel articles to help fund their adventures. Before long they moved into authoring books and in 1995 established Boiling Billy Publications to write and publish accurate and up-to-date guidebooks for people who, like themselves, love travelling and exploring Australia's great outdoors.

As part of their ongoing field research schedule, they generally camp out around 100 nights each year in various campsites from the coast to the deserts. Tasmania remains one of their favourite states for going camping.

When not on the road travelling (that's the fun part), their home base is on a secluded farm, tucked away high up on the coastal escarpment in the Monaro region of New South Wales, looking out over the Brogo Wilderness in Wadbilliga National Park.

Craig and Cathy's website is at www.boilingbilly.net.au

Contents

Dove Lake and Cradle Mountain

Regional Map of Tasmania

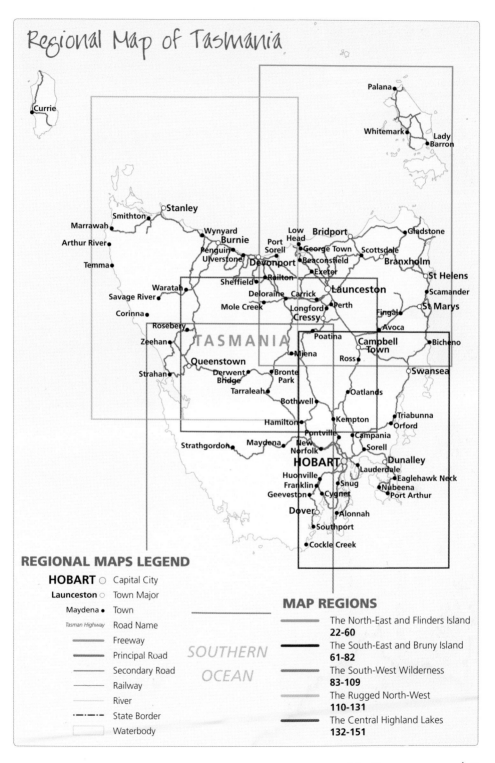

REGIONAL MAPS LEGEND

HOBART ○	Capital City
Launceston ○	Town Major
Maydena ●	Town
Tasman Highway	Road Name
	Freeway
	Principal Road
	Secondary Road
	Railway
	River
–·–·–·–	State Border
▭	Waterbody

MAP REGIONS

The North-East and Flinders Island
22-60

The South-East and Bruny Island
61-82

The South-West Wilderness
83-109

The Rugged North-West
110-131

The Central Highland Lakes
132-151

How to use this Guide

Camping Guide to Tasmania is designed in an easy to use format that makes finding that perfect campsite simple. The guide has been broken into five different chapters covering the major tourism regions throughout Tasmania.

In this book, each park, forest or reserve throughout the state that allows camping has its own entry. You can locate their approximate positions on the regional maps at the beginning of each chapter. These maps provide an overview of the region covered in the chapter and provide a starting reference point. There are also a number of more detailed maps for some of the national parks, forests and reserves throughout the guide. The grey boxes on the regional maps at the start of each region show the area covered by these maps in that region.

Each entry, whether it be a national park, forest reserve or riverside area, has detailed information relating to that site including access details, map references (MR) and some include GPS coordinates. These map references refer to the Touring Maps section and are useful for locating the campsite. For example, MR: Map 8 J4 refers to Touring Map 8 and the grid reference is J4 – this is the location of River and Rocks camping area in Moulting Lagoon Game Reserve.

We use symbols to detail the facilities and activities at each site.

We also include Further Information boxes for the authority to contact for making enquiries or bookings, along with prices and other details that apply to the camping site.

Although all care has been taken when compiling this guide and is correct at the time of going to print, note that conditions at campsites are constantly changing. Camping fees may be introduced to previously free areas or may be increased from what is listed. Some areas may also be closed from time to time – fire and flood, for example, can have a marked affect on an area literally overnight.

Note for GPS Users

A substantial number of campsites in this guide have coordinates (latitude and longitude) which can be utilized by those with GPS receivers as an additional means of navigating to the campsite. The coordinates were acquired during field research using GDA 94 map datum and are in HDDD MM.MMM format.

Remember

After you have chosen your campsite we strongly recommend that you contact the park, forest or reserve office prior to your departure to obtain advice on current and upcoming conditions. For sites where a camping/entry fee is payable we recommend that you contact the land managers to obtain the current fee schedule before arrival. Be aware that some sites may require advance bookings, especially during the popular holiday periods over Christmas/ New Year and Easter. Booking requirements are detailed for these sites in the guide.

Camping in Tasmania

Tasmania is one of Australia's best state-based destinations for going camping. Now becoming increasingly popular with both interstate and overseas visitors alike, Tasmania is no longer one of Australia's best kept secrets. The word's out and people are now holidaying in the 'Island State' in unprecedented numbers, many travelling around in caravans, campervans and motorhomes. With a host of superb campsites ranging from idyllic coastal locations to secluded lakeside sites up in the Central Highlands, campers are sure to find the ideal site to pitch their tent or setup a van.

Camping is fun and a great way to experience Tasmania. Here you'll find something to suit everyone, whether you're a once a year camper, a long term traveller, an avid adventurer, a bushwalker or out four-wheel drive touring. Now in its fully updated fourth edition, Camping Guide to Tasmania is your comprehensive guide to camping within Tasmania's national parks, conservation areas, forest reserves and lakeside reserves. It contains details on the state's designated campsites where you can enjoy a night under the stars. From the rugged south-west wilderness to the picturesque east coast to the unique central highland lakes, there are parks and reserves that cater for all styles of camping amongst some of Australia's most beautiful and diverse landscapes. This compact state sure does offer a lot of variety for visitors to experience.

No matter what type of camping you prefer, be it a secluded walk-in campsite, car-based camping beside a river or the ocean, or with your van at a campground with amenities, you will be sure to find an ideal campsite to suit your needs amongst the 180 plus sites in this guide. You will find opportunities to relax on one of the many beautiful white sandy beaches with crystal clear water on the east coast, walk amongst the treetops and lookout over the mighty Huon River at the Tahune Forest AirWalk, take a cruise on one of the west coast's picturesque waterways, fish for trout in one of the many inland lakes and visit historic towns with rich and colourful pasts. Visitors can walk through world renown wilderness regions, marvel at the abundant wildlife including Tasmania's own devil and be captivated by towering forests. All this and much more is available in the 96 parks and reserves within this guide.

So, why not pack the tent and head off to discover the delights of Tasmania. See spectacular plants and wildlife in their natural environments (many of which are unique to Tasmania), take in the sights and sounds of the Tasmanian bush and gaze in awe at the stunning natural beauty that is to be found throughout Australia's visually spectacular island state.

Happy Camping

Craig Lewis and Cathy Savage
Kybeyan NSW

Getting to Tasmania

The majority of people travelling to Tasmania for a camping holiday either bring their own vehicle from the mainland via the Spirit of Tasmania ferry service or fly-drive, that is, fly to Tasmania and hire a campervan or motorhome. The advantage of travelling on the ferry service is that you have your own vehicle with your own camping kit.

The *Spirit of Tasmania I* and *II* travel between Melbourne and Devonport daily, leaving both Melbourne and Devonport (on days of single sailings) early evening (7.30pm) for the 10 hour overnight crossing and arrive in port early next morning (6.30am). On days of dual sailings (both day and overnight) departures are at 9pm and arrival at 7am next morning. During summer (Jan – April) there are also scheduled day sailings which leave at 9am and arrive at 7pm. You have the choice (for a cost) of a variety of sleeper cabins or 'aircraft' style sit-up seats for overnight sailings. For day sailings, you grab a seat anywhere - either inside or on deck. The ferries leave from Station Pier on Port Phillip Bay (it is well signposted) in Melbourne and from the ferry terminal at East Devonport, which is on the opposite side of the river from the main part of town.

You need to book in advance for these ferries, you can't just show up and expect to hop aboard. If travelling during the peak summer months be sure to book your passage well in advance as often the ships are fully booked for certain crossings months ahead.

There are a few issues travelling campers should be aware of when boarding the ferries. Gas bottles which are not fixed to either the vehicle or trailer must be removed and placed in the separate bottle trailer and retrieved upon disembarking. All fuel containers (jerry cans) must be emptied of fuel and filled with water, otherwise they will not be permitted on board the vessel. These will be checked at boarding. When arriving in Tasmania quarantine inspections occur and restrictions apply to carrying fresh fruit and vegetables and fresh fish products, plants and soil. These products will be confiscated.

FURTHER Information

Fares, sailing schedules, booking and further details can be had by contacting TT Lines on 1800 634 906 or online at www.spiritoftasmania.com.au
Quarantine Hotline: Dept Primary Industries, Parks, Water and Environment 1800 084 881 or 03 6233 3352 and www.dpiw.tas.gov.au and follow the quarantine links.

Planning

Like many experienced campers, we've found over the years the key to hassle free camping is to follow the KIS principal – Keep It Simple. It's all about getting back to basics, enjoying the great Australian outdoors. Stick to the basics. Travel light.

Your camping holiday will be much more enjoyable with the right gear. If you are setting up a camping outfit then buy the best gear you can afford. Quality gear, such as tents and sleeping gear will serve you well over a long period if looked after.

The warmer months of the year, from around October through to April are the best times for camping along Tasmania's coastal fringe. Days are generally warm and nights mild, although Tasmania can experience the odd spell of hot weather across the state over the summer period. Remember to always pack a warm jumper and long pants, even in summer. The Highlands and Central Lakes region is popular over summer, especially with fisherfolk who flock to the numerous waterside campsites. Try the shoulder seasons here for fewer crowds. The South-West region of the state can experience extreme temperatures during winter with periods of cold wet weather and is best avoided at this time. Spring, summer and early autumn are the best times to visit here, especially if bushwalking.

Riting insects such as spiders, bees, wasps, ants, ticks or mosquitoes can turn a dream camping holiday into a nightmare. To help protect yourself from these unwelcome visitors wear long pants, long sleeve shirts and shoes and don't forget insect repellent.

Never pitch your tent directly under large trees. Those large, shady trees lining our inland rivers might look like inviting campsites but they have a habit of dropping branches without warning.

When planning your camping trip, don't head off without:

- Good maps. See 'Maps, guidebooks and passes' in this section. If you plan on venturing off the beaten track, be it bushwalking, vehicle touring or fishing, be sure to carry a detailed map of the area you plan to visit.
- A gas/liquid fuel stove. If the campsite you want to visit doesn't allow you to light a fire (be aware of summer fire restrictions across the state) or provide cooking facilities, then you will need to take your own. A small single burner gas stove is fine for 2-3 people; 2 burner stoves are a better option for families.
- Insect repellent and a first aid kit. Mosquitoes, sand flies and bugs can be a nuisance while a good first aid kit is a necessity.

- Wet weather protection. Besides personal wet weather gear, a poly tarp can be rigged up to provide protection from rain and wind.
- Plenty of fresh drinking water. Carry water with you on walks, even short ones
- If you are camping in remote areas well away from shops be sure to take enough food with you – and always pack for an extra day or two in case inclement weather etc holds you up. When you're out in the fresh air, you often have a bigger appetite, especially if you combine some swimming, bike riding or bushwalking. Kids especially get very hungry on camping trips, so make sure you include healthy nibbles.

For a detailed equipment checklist see the Equipment Checklist section.

WE COULDN'T live without...

We always travel with a 12 volt portable fridge, and have done so for the last 15 years. We have used a number of different brands over the years and have found them all to be efficient and reliable. Our current fridge is a Waeco 50 litre unit. We have our meat vacuum sealed, so run the fridge as a refrigerator, not as a freezer. Visit www.waeco.com.au

One of the best portable barbecues we have come across is the *Biji Barbi*. It consists of a round steel plate with a slight dish to allow the fat and oil to run to the centre and drip through a small hole, adding fuel to your cooking fire. There are three folding legs as well as a folding handle. The Biji Barbi is a permanent piece of our bush cooking gear. Check out www.biji-barbi.com.au

Under Cover

There is a bewildering choice of camping accommodation available today, be it a tent, camper trailer, caravan, swag or roof top tent. Your choice of camping accommodation really depends on things such as the time you'll spend using it, your budget, available vehicle space (whether it is to be stowed in the vehicle, on a roof rack or towed), the number of people to accommodate and the environment it will be used in. With the increasing use of four-wheel drives as towing vehicles, camper trailers are gaining in popularity at an amazing pace, especially the more rugged off-road units. These are often favoured by long term travellers and families who camp out regularly. Advantages of camper trailers include extra storage space, comfortable sleeping area and often extra shade and weather cover from awnings. Remember though that some destinations are out of bounds or just not practical if you are towing a trailer. Becoming increasingly more common are the number of national park campsites throughout the state which are not trailer friendly. These sites are ringed by bollards, providing a small vehicle parking space. You carry your camping gear over these to the grassed campsite.

Sleep Easy

Self-inflating camp mattresses are by far the best choice for tent-based campers and offer a comfortable nights sleep. Mattresses range from ultra light ¾ length models for bushwalkers through to heavier and more bulky double models which are perfect for vehicle based campers. We use a double self-inflating mattress in our tent, and it also doubles as our swag mattress. Self-inflating mattresses roll up to form a compact cylinder which can easily be stowed in your vehicle, or on a roof rack. Although they rarely leak, don't forget a puncture repair kit just in case. Comfortable bedding is also a must. Winter nights in Tasmania can fall below freezing, the weather is very changeable across the state's far west coast while summer on the south-east coast is far more temperate. A good, zero degrees rated sleeping bag will cover most camping scenarios. We use sleeping bags when bushwalking but prefer sheets and a doona when vehicle-based camping. And don't forget your pillow.

Now I See the Light

The quality and choice of camp lighting has improved a lot in recent years. While gas (LPG or butane) lanterns are still popular, we have found the portable 12 volt fluorescent lights to be the best all-round camp lighting. These units throw out good light with minimal current draw from your vehicle's battery. Rechargeable lanterns are another option (they can be recharged via your vehicles cigarette lighter socket) while a rechargeable torch or two takes up little room. We also take with us a good quality headlamp which is indispensible for cooking and other late night camp chores.

Lets Cook

An increasing number of national park campgrounds have gas/electric barbecues for visitor use. If you would like a campfire and a camping area has a wood fireplace then please use it – and keep your cooking fire small. A folding grate for the fire and a BBQ plate (some camping areas provide these), frying pan, a few pots with lids and a couple of billies and maybe a camp oven is all that's required for camp cooking. A pair of sturdy leather gloves and shovel are also handy. And don't forget a gas stove.

MAPS, PASSES AND PERMITS

All campsites in this guide are referenced to the Touring Map section in the back of the book (abbreviated to MR in campsite descriptions). This road atlas, which covers Tasmania in detail, is used to locate campsites along with the regional maps and national park/forest maps in this guide.

For those who require greater detail the Tasmanian Government publishes a series of four 1:250 000 scale topographic maps that cover the whole state. These are titled North-West, North-East, South-East and South-West.

There are a range of handy guides available to regional areas of Tasmania, some detailing the states top outdoor locations. Two invaluable guides for campers include National Parks, Forests & Waterways Tasmania, A Visitors Guide and Tasmania's Great Short Walks - 60 Walks Around Tasmania. These and other guides are available free from visitor information centres aboard the Spirit of Tasmania ferries as well as centres throughout Tasmania.

National Park Annual Passes

Entry fees apply to visit national parks throughout Tasmania. There are a range of park passes available to visitors, the Holiday Pass offers excellent value for visitors to the state as it covers all national parks and is valid for up to eight weeks. This pass is available for vehicle based travellers, motorcycle tourers and even those visiting on foot. Please note that the Parks Passes do not cover camping fees and/or overnight walking track fees. The Passes are available from Parks and Wildlife offices, at self-registration stations at major parks and at various other outlets including aboard the Spirit of Tasmania ferries.

For further details on the range of Park Passes available contact the individual Parks and Wildlife Service office listed in this guide, or Parks and Wildlife Tasmania head office on 1300 135 513. Alternatively, log onto the Parks and Wildlife Service Tasmania website at www.parks.tas.gov.au

Fishing

Fishing licences are required in Tasmania, contact the appropriate department for up-to-date information on licensing, rules and regulations. Sea Fisheries - Department of Primary Industry, Water and Environment Tel: 03 6233 7042 or visit their website at www.fishing.tas.gov.au

Inland Fisheries Service Tel: 03 6261 8050 or visit the sevice's website at www.ifs.tas.gov.au

Camping Permits and Fees

Camping fees and permits are required for a number of campsites in this guide. Camping fees in national parks are generally geared to the level of facilities provided at the campsite. Depending on the campsite, fees may be payable when booking, be collected by a caretaker or be payable at a self-registration station at the site. Details on fees and permits can be found in the Further Information box for that listing, along with payment details.

For safety purposes, some remote walk-in sites or canoe access sites may require visitors to register their intentions with the land managers.

NOTE on camping fees

> The camping fees indicated in the Further Information box are correct at the time of research and generally reflect the low season fee. Peak season fees may be higher than those listed. Camping fees may rise or be introduced to areas which may have previously been free of charge. It is the responsibility of individuals to enquire with the land managers about the status of areas they wish to visit, including current fees, prior to departure.

FIRE WARNINGS AND RESTRICTIONS

On days declared total fire bans you're not allowed to have any fire in the open, this includes solid fuel fires, gas cookers or barbecues. Fire bans are generally broadcast on local radio stations and it's your responsibility to be aware of these. On days of high fire danger it may be prudent to refrain from having open fires; use gas or fuel cooking appliances instead.

To protect the natural environment and local wildlife, you may find that a number of national parks and reserves listed in this guide do not permit campfires. For these parks and reserves, it's essential that you carry your own gas/fuel stove for cooking.

Bushfires

During the bushfire season, which is generally early November to late April in Tasmania, it is vital to be fire smart. If you are out camping and a bushfire threatens seek shelter, be it in a river, stream, dam, large clearing or behind a rock outcrop and prepare a shelter from the fire's radiant heat. Keep down low to the ground and cover up. Remember, it isn't wise to try and outrun a bushfire – shelter until the main fire front has passed. Check out the Tasmania Fire Service website at www.fire.tas.gov.au for additional bushfire information.

Firewood

Wood is becoming scarce in popular camping areas. Fallen and dead timer also provides habitats for the local wildlife. If you're camping where campfires are permitted, try to purchase or collect your wood prior to arrival to the campsite. Some parks prohibit the collection of firewood within the park and some parks may have signposted firewood collection points outside the park boundary. Also, to help protect the spread of exotic weeds and pests, some national parks and reserves request that collected firewood from outside the immediate area is not to be taken into the parks.

Vegetation

Please do not cut down any vegetation, either living or dead, and do not collect or use wood that may have habitat holes. If you use a campfire you must ensure that all combustible material is clear for 4 metres, never leave the campfire unattended and always put it out with water (never with sand or dirt). Never throw cans or glass into your campfire.

Remember the average-sized campfire...

- is capable of generating over 500 Degrees of heat after burning for only three hours.
- when extinguished with sand or dirt, retains up to 100 Degrees of heat for eight hours.
- when extinguished with a bucket of water retains little or no heat after of period of ten minutes.

FURTHER Information

> **Tasmanian Fire Service (total fireban updates and bushfire updates)**
> **Tel:** 1800 000 699 or 03 6230 8600
> **Web:** www.fire.tas.gov.au
> All fire emergencies dial 000

GREYWATER AND SULLAGE DUMP SITES

Dumps sites may be used by caravanners, campervanners and motorhomers to conveniently dispose of greywater & chemical toilet sullage. Greywater and sullage should never be emptied into composting or pit toilets, as chemicals destroy the composting bacteria, rendering them ineffective.

- **Arthur River:** Airey Street, (Gardner Point) Edge of the World
- **Beaconsfield:** Showgrounds, Grubb Street
- **Bicheno:** Bicheno Beach opposite police station, Champ Street
- **Bridport:** Bridport Caravan Park, Bentley Street
- **Brighton:** Brighton Hotel, Midlands Highway
- Burnie: Cooee Point Reserve, Cooee Point Road
- **Cambridge:** Cambridge Memorial Oval, Cambridge Road
- **Campbell Town:** King Street Oval
- **Cygnet:** Burtons Reserve, off Charlton Street
- **Deloraine:** Adjacent to racecourse entry, Racecourse Drive
- **Devonport East:** Girdlestone Park Football Ground, cnr John & Caroline Streets
- **Dover:** Kent Beach Road
- **Evandale:** Morven Park, Barclay Street
- **Fingal:** located at public toilets in Talbot Street
- **Franklin:** Franklin Foreshore camping and caravan area A6 highway – see page 69
- **George Town:** Visitor Information Centre, Main Street
- **Kempton:** red toilet block at rear of Victoria Hall, Main Street
- **Kingston:** Kingston Wetlands Park, access behind Kingston Hotel at corner of Channel Hwy
- **Latrobe:** car park off Cotton Street behind supermarkets
- **Launceston:** Treasure Island Caravan Park, 94 Glen Dhu Street
- **Longford:** Riverside Caravan Park, Archer Street
- **Narawntapu National Park:** Located at Bakers Point camping area – see page 47
- **Oatlands:** Junction of Williams and Wellington Streets
- **Penguin:** corner Main and Johnsons Beach roads.
- **Pontville:** Pontville Park, Midlands Highway
- **Port Arthur:** Port Arthur Caravan Park at Garden Point, turn left off highway before town
- **Port Sorell:** Port Sorell Jetty Point
- **Rosny:** Sewage Treatment Plant off Rosny Esplande
- **Scottsdale:** North East Park Campground, A3 Highway – see page 52
- **Sheffield:** West Nook Road
- **Sorell:** Council depot, Montague Street (weekdays only)
- **St Helens:** Sportsgrounds, off Tully Street
- **St Helens:** St Helens Caravan Park, Penelope Street
- **Stanley:** Stanley Caravan Park, Wharf Road
- **Stanley:** Tatlows Beach off Wharf Road
- **Swansea:** Opposite post office at boat ramp car park, Jetty Road
- **Triabunna:** Visitor Information Centre, Cnr Charles Street and The Esplanade
- **Ulverstone:** Apex Caravan Park, Queen Street
- **Ulverstone:** end of Victoria Street near beach.
- **Waratah:** opposite Waratah Council works depot, Annie Street
- **Westbury:** Andy's Motorhome and Camper Park, Meander Valley Road – see page 35
- **Wynyard:** Wynyard Solid Waste Transfer Station, Goldie Street – 9am to 5pm seven days

TREADING SOFTLY ON TASMANIA

Tasmania's parks and reserves are some of the state's most precious and at the same time sensitive recreational resources.

When enjoying these areas, whether it be camping, walking, canoeing, cycling, car touring, 4WDing or just going bush, it's important to tread lightly on the environment.

Minimal impact camping is the way to go. When setting up camp there are a few simple guidelines, which if followed ensure that Tasmania's parks and reserves are preserved for everyone to enjoy in the future.

Minimal impact camping guidelines:

 Be prepared: Plan your trip carefully and make sure your gear is in good order (for good gear tips, see 'Planning' in this section).

 Camp fire safety: Use fireplaces where provided and observe any fire bans. Clear combustible material 4 metres away from the fire. Be sure the fire is out before leaving (for more, see the section 'Fire Warnings and Restrictions').

 Protect plants and animals: Protect plants and animals: If possible, make your camp to avoid trampling plants or disturbing animals. Do not feed wildlife as 'human food' can cause illness and disease to animals.

 Waterway care: Don't pollute waterways. Don't use soap or detergents in or close to waterways. Wash at least 100 metres from waterways.

 Toilet time: Use toilets if provided. If not, bury wastes at least 100 metres away from campsites and watercourses, in a hole at least 15cm deep.

 Use rubbish bins if provided or take your rubbish with you when you leave. Don't bury rubbish. Leave campsites better than you found them.

 Neighbours: Be considerate of others when camping nearby.

WHAT TO PACK

Camping Equipment

- ❏ Bucket
- ❏ Chairs
- ❏ Dust pan & brush
- ❏ First Aid Kit
- ❏ Fluro light
- ❏ Ground sheet
- ❏ Head torch
- ❏ Mattress/s
- ❏ Mattress pump
- ❏ Pillows and cases
- ❏ Screen/mesh tent
- ❏ Sleeping bag
- ❏ Spare rope
- ❏ Swag
- ❏ Table
- ❏ Tent
- ❏ Tent pegs
- ❏ Tent poles
- ❏ Tent rope
- ❏ Torch
- ❏ Torch batteries
- ❏ Water container

Cooking Equipment

- ❏ Matches and/or lighter
- ❏ Firelighters
- ❏ Two burner gas stove and gas bottle
- ❏ BBQ plate
- ❏ Grill or grate
- ❏ 2 saucepans with lids
- ❏ Frying pan
- ❏ Camp oven

- ❏ Trivet - to fit camp oven
- ❏ Billy
- ❏ Tripod hanger and hooks
- ❏ Pie dish - to fit camp oven
- ❏ Pizza tray - to fit camp oven
- ❏ Camp oven lifters
- ❏ Shovel - long handled
- ❏ Leather gloves

Miscellaneous Cooking Items

- ❏ Roll of aluminium foil
- ❏ Roll of cling wrap
- ❏ Paper towel
- ❏ Plastic bottle for milk
- ❏ Plastic bottle for cordial
- ❏ Plastic bottle for extra water
- ❏ Storage containers with lids
- ❏ Zip lock bags

Personal Eating Equipment - 1 per person

- ❏ Bowl
- ❏ Fork
- ❏ Knife
- ❏ Mug
- ❏ Plate
- ❏ Spoon
- ❏ Steak Knife
- ❏ Tea spoon

Cooking Utensils

- ❏ Mixing bowls
- ❏ Measuring jug
- ❏ Tongs - short or long
- ❏ Bar-B-Q Mate
- ❏ Basting brush

- ❏ Serving spoon
- ❏ Slotted serving spoon
- ❏ Peelers
- ❏ Egg flip
- ❏ Flat grater
- ❏ Can opener with bottle opener
- ❏ Swiss Army Knife
- ❏ Flat Strainer
- ❏ Egg rings
- ❏ Large sharp knife
- ❏ Bread/Serrated edge knife
- ❏ Wooden spoons
- ❏ Cutting board
- ❏ Mesh toaster
- ❏ Measuring spoon and/or tablespoon
- ❏ Extra plate and bowl for serving
- ❏ General purpose scissors

Washing/Cleaning Equipment

- ❏ Cloth
- ❏ Clothesline and pegs
- ❏ Detergent
- ❏ Dish brush
- ❏ Garbage bags
- ❏ Scourer
- ❏ Scrubbing brush
- ❏ Sponge
- ❏ Tea towel/s
- ❏ Wash up bucket
- ❏ Washing powder for clothes

Personal Items

- ❏ Comb and/or brush
- ❏ Toothbrush
- ❏ Toothpaste
- ❏ Towel
- ❏ Face Washer
- ❏ Soap and container
- ❏ Shampoo and Conditioner
- ❏ Deodorant
- ❏ Sunblock
- ❏ Toilet paper
- ❏ Insect repellent

USEFUL RESOURCES AND CONTACTS

Parks & Wildlife Service
Tel: 1300 135 513
Web: www.parks.tas.gov.au

Parks & Wildlife Service Visitor Centres - Open 7 days
Cradle Mountain Tel: 03 6492 1110
Freycinet Tel: 03 6256 7000
Hastings Caves Tel: 03 6298 3209
Lake St Clair Tel: 03 6289 1172
Mt Field Tel: 03 6288 1149
Narawntapu Tel: 03 6428 6277

Forestry Tasmania
Tel: 03 6233 8203
Web: www.forestrytas.com.au

Hydro Tasmania
Tel: 1300 360 441
Web: www.hydro.com.au

Inland Fisheries Service
Tel: 03 6261 8050 or 1300 INFISH
Web: www.ifs.tas.gov.au

Department of Primary Industries, Parks, Water & Environment - Sea Fishing & Aquaculture
Recreational Fisheries Enquiries
Tel: 03 6233 7042
Web: www.fishing.tas.gov.au

Tasmanian Fire Service
Tel: 1800 000 699 or 03 6230 8600
Web: www.fire.tas.gov.au

RACT
Roadside Assistance **Tel:** 131 111
General Enquiries **Tel:** 132 722
Web: www.ract.com.au

Transport Tasmania
General Enquiries **Tel:** 1300 851 225
Web: www.transport.tas.gov.au

Tourism Tasmania
Tel: 1300 827 743
Web: www.discovertasmania.com.au

Regional Visitor Information Centres

Hobart
Tel: 03 6238 4222
Web: www.hobarttravelcentre.com.au

Launceston
Tel: 03 6336 3133

Devonport
Tel: 03 6424 4466
Web: www.devonporttasmania.travel

Burnie
Tel: 03 6434 6111

Deloraine
Tel: 03 6362 3471
Web: www.greatwesterntiers.net.au

Exeter
Tel: 1800 637 989
Web: www.tamarvalley.com.au

Geeveston
Tel: 03 6297 1821 or 03 6297 1836
Web: www.forestandheritagecentre.com.au

George Town
Tel: 03 6382 1700
Web: www.tamarvalley.com.au

Huonville
Tel: 03 6264 1838

Kettering
Tel: 03 6267 4494

Oatlands
Tel: 03 6254 1212

Port Arthur Historic Site
Tel: 03 6251 2371

Ross
Tel: 03 6381 5466

Scottsdale
Tel: 03 6352 6520

Sheffield
Tel: 03 6491 1036

Stanley
Tel: 03 6458 1330

St Helens
Tel: 03 6376 1744

Strahan
Tel: 03 6472 6800

Triabunna
Tel: 03 6257 4772

Ulverstone
Tel: 03 6425 2839

Wynyard
Tel: 03 6443 8330

Spirit of Tasmania (TT-Line)
Information and Reservations **Tel:** 1800 634 906
Web: www.spiritoftasmania.com.au

Bureau of Meterology
Web: www.bom.gov.au

Edgar Campground, Southwest National Park

The North-East and Flinders Island

ONE OF TASMANIA'S MOST VISITED regions, the North-East is blessed with kilometre after kilometre of stunning coastline which features pristine white sandy beaches interspersed with rugged headlands and rocky outcrops. Popular locations include the Bay of Fires Conservation Area north of St Helens and Mt William National Park, one of the North-East's more remote and beautiful national parks. At both of these locations you will find a host of picture-perfect coastal campsites.

BEST Campsites!

Stumpys Bay: Campsite No 2
Mt William National Park

Griffin camping area
Saddleback Plantation

Cosy Corner North camping area
Bay of Fires Conservation Area

Waterhouse Point camping area
Waterhouse Conservation Area

Bakers Point camping area
Narawntapu National Park

In the north of the region and fronting Bass Strait is the delightful holiday destination of Bridport, while running to the north-east is Waterhouse Conservation Area—a popular fishing and camping destination over summer. This park, which offers minimal visitor facilities, offers ten camping areas to choose from, ranging from protected lakeside sites to those on headlands with stunning ocean vistas. Further to the west near Port Sorell is Narawntapu National Park, a great spot for wildlife watching. This park is also located on the coast and has ocean access as well as a protected estuary.

Away from the coast is the winter playground of Ben Lomond National Park, which offers camping while a little to the north is the delightful Griffin camping area in Saddleback Plantation. Situated beside the South Esk River, it is popular with anglers, mountain bikers and trail bike riders.

As opposed to most of Tasmania it is possible to enjoy this region all year round with its mild climate. Here you will find the warmer months tend to be the most pleasant, especially the coastal parks and reserves where campsites are at a premium over the peak summer period, as both locals and visitors flock to the region.

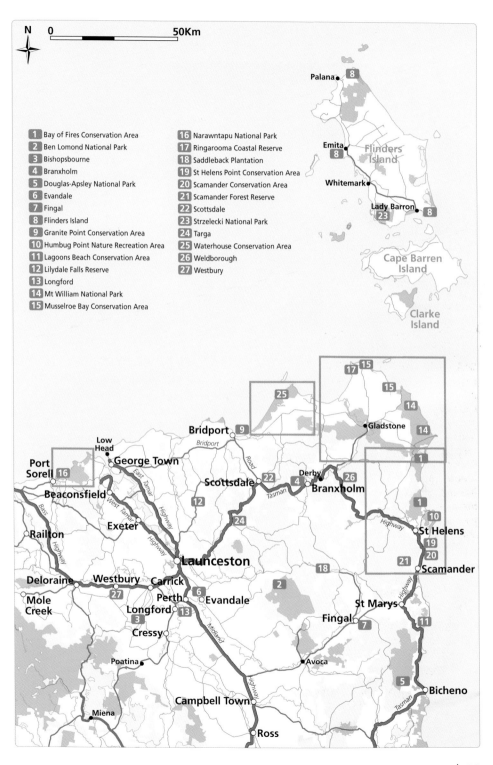

N 0 _____ 50Km

1 Bay of Fires Conservation Area
2 Ben Lomond National Park
3 Bishopsbourne
4 Branxholm
5 Douglas-Apsley National Park
6 Evandale
7 Fingal
8 Flinders Island
9 Granite Point Conservation Area
10 Humbug Point Nature Recreation Area
11 Lagoons Beach Conservation Area
12 Lilydale Falls Reserve
13 Longford
14 Mt William National Park
15 Musselroe Bay Conservation Area

16 Narawntapu National Park
17 Ringarooma Coastal Reserve
18 Saddleback Plantation
19 St Helens Point Conservation Area
20 Scamander Conservation Area
21 Scamander Forest Reserve
22 Scottsdale
23 Strzelecki National Park
24 Targa
25 Waterhouse Conservation Area
26 Weldborough
27 Westbury

Palana 8

Emita 8
Flinders Island

Whitemark

Lady Barron
23 8

Cape Barren Island

Clarke Island

17 15

25

15

14

Gladstone 14

Bridport 9

Bridport

Low Head

Port Sorell 16

George Town

East Tamar

West Tamar

Scottsdale 22

Derby 4
Branxholm

Tasman

26

1

1

10

St Helens
19
20

Highway

Beaconsfield

12

Bass Highway

Exeter

Railton

24

Launceston

18

21

Scamander

Deloraine

Westbury
27

Carrick

Perth 6

Evandale

2

Mole Creek

Longford 13

3

Cressy

Midland

St Marys

Fingal 7

5

Highway

11

Poatina

Avoca

Bicheno

Campbell Town

Tasman

Ross

The southern section of the conservation area stretches along the coast from Binalong Bay in the south for 13km north to The Gardens. Located along this pristine coastline are numerous camping areas signposted off The Gardens Road, which is signposted 8km north of St Helens along Binalong Bay Road. Further north Policemans Point is situated to the south of Ansons Bay and accessed via Ansons Bay Road. The area's magnificent coastline, spectacular views, beautiful beaches and azure waters make it a popular destination for swimmers, divers and fisherfolk.

NORTHERN CAMPING AREA

Policemans Point Campground

Policemans Point is situated 5.2km east of the C843 road. Southern access from St Helens, take the C843/Ansons Bay Road for 34.5km, then take signposted road to Policemans Point. Northern access from Ansons Bay take the C843/St Helens Road 3km west of Ansons Bay, travel for 5.1km to the signposted Policemans Point road. Campsites are protected in coastal heath on the southern side of Ansons Bay mouth. Bring drinking water, firewood and chemical toilet.

GPS S:41 03.680 E:148 17.425
MR: Map 4 J5

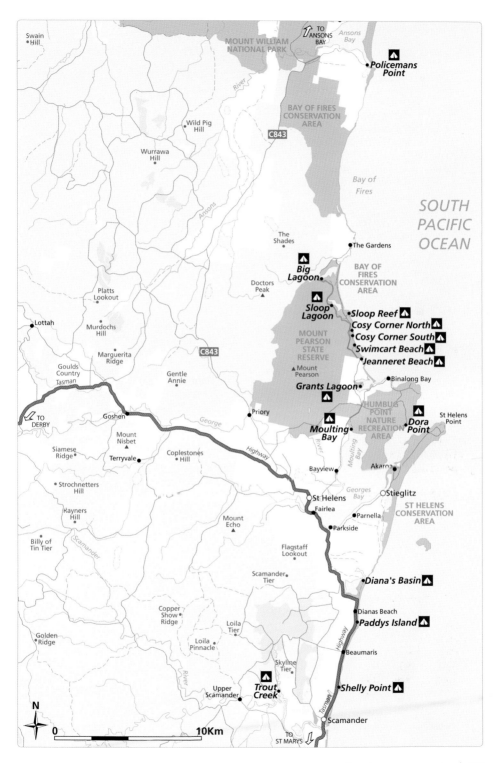

Swain Hill

TO ANSONS BAY

Ansons Bay

MOUNT WILLIAM NATIONAL PARK

Policemans Point

BAY OF FIRES CONSERVATION AREA

C843

Wild Pig Hill

Wurrawa Hill

River

Ansons

Bay of Fires

SOUTH PACIFIC OCEAN

The Shades

The Gardens

Big Lagoon

Doctors Peak

BAY OF FIRES CONSERVATION AREA

Platts Lookout

Lottah

Murdochs Hill

Marguerita Ridge

Sloop Lagoon

MOUNT PEARSON STATE RESERVE

Mount Pearson

Sloop Reef
Cosy Corner North
Cosy Corner South
Swimcart Beach
Jeanneret Beach

Goulds Country

Tasman

C843

Gentle Annie

Grants Lagoon

Binalong Bay

TO DERBY

Goshen

George

Priory

HUMBUG POINT NATURE RECREATION AREA

Dora Point

St Helens Point

Mount Nisbet

Moulting Bay

Siamese Ridge

Terryvale

Coplestones Hill

Highway

Bayview

Moulting Bay

Akaroa

Strochnetters Hill

Georges Bay

Stieglitz

Rayners Hill

Mount Echo

St Helens

Fairlea

Parnella

ST HELENS CONSERVATION AREA

Billy of Tin Tier

Scamander

Parkside

Flagstaff Lookout

Scamander Tier

Diana's Basin

Copper Show Ridge

Loila Tier

Dianas Beach

Paddys Island

Golden Ridge

Loila Pinnacle

Beaumaris

River

Skyline Tier

Upper Scamander

Trout Creek

Highway

Shelly Point

N

Tasman

0   10Km

Scamander

TO ST MARYS

SOUTHERN CAMPING AREAS

Grants Lagoon camping area

Signposted access off The Gardens Road, 1.3km from Binalong Bay Road. Number of grassed clearings set back from water. Little shade. Suitable for big rigs. Bring drinking water and firewood.

GPS S:41 15.256 E:148 17.372
MR: Map 4 J6

Jeanneret Beach camping area

Signposted access off The Gardens Road, 3.2km from Binalong Bay Road. Bring drinking water and firewood.

GPS S:41 14.260 E:148 17.403
MR: Map 4 J6

Swimcart Beach camping area

Signposted access off The Gardens Road, 4.1km from Binalong Bay Road. Then in 400m to sites. Suitable for big rigs. Bring drinking water and firewood.

GPS S:41 13.743 E:148 17.047
MR: Map 4 J6

Cosy Corner South camping area

Signposted access off The Gardens Road, 5.3km from Binalong Bay Road. Then in 200m to sites. Number of sites along the coast and other sites set back in vegetation. Bring drinking water and firewood.

GPS S:41 13.419 E:148 16.966
MR: Map 4 J6

Cosy Corner South camping area

Cosy Corner North camping area

Signposted access off The Gardens Road, 5.6km from Binalong Bay Road. Then in 200m to sites. Best suited for larger vans and big rigs. Bring drinking water and firewood.

GPS S:41 13.250 E:148 16.907
MR: Map 4 J6

Sloop Reef camping area

Signposted access off The Gardens Road, 7.4km from Binalong Bay Road. Then 400m to crossroads. At crossroads road on left leads 200m to small camping area overlooking the water suitable for camper trailers and small vans. At crossroads road on right leads 200m to small camping area suitable for tent based camping. Bring drinking water, firewood and chemical toilet.

Area for camper trailers and small vans **GPS** S:41 12.547 E:148 16.728
Area for tents **GPS** S:41 12.736 E:148 16.843
MR: Map 4 J6

Sloop Lagoon camping area

Access via Old Gardens Road which is signposted off The Gardens Road, 6.3km from Binalong Bay Road. Numerous tracks off Old Gardens Road lead to bush campsites on the lagoon's shore. Bring drinking water, firewood and chemical toilet.

MR: Map 4 J6

Big Lagoon camping area

Access off The Gardens Road, 2km north of the bridge over Sloop Lagoon. Then drive in for 1km to the turn-off into Bay of Fires Conservation Area. Numerous tracks lead to bush campsites on the lagoon's shore. Bring drinking water, firewood and chemical toilet.

MR: Map 4 J6

FURTHER Information

Parks & Wildlife Service St Helens
Tel: 03 6376 1550
St Helens Visitor Centre
Tel: 03 6376 1744
Parks Pass: Not required.
Maximum stay: 4 weeks.

Cosy Corner camping area

2 Ben Lomond National Park

The Ben Lomond plateau is a popular winter destination for skiers and in summer for bushwalkers, birdwatchers and nature enthusiasts. The park is located 50km south-east of Launceston. Signposted access to the park is via the Ben Lomond Road off the C401, 13km south of Upper Blessington.

Ben Lomond camping area

Access via Ben Lomond Road, 13km south of Upper Blessington. Camping area located 1km within park boundary with six unpowered sites. Best suited for tent-based camping, small trailers and campervans. Bring firewood. Gas/fuel stove preferred.

GPS S:41 30.250 E:147 36.767
MR: Map 4 G8

Bush camping

Remote bush camping for self-sufficient bushwalkers. Contact ranger for details.

FURTHER Information

> **Parks & Wildlife Service Prospect**
> **Tel:** 03 6336 5397
> **Parks Pass:** Required.

3 Bishopsbourne

The quaint village of Bishopsbourne was built on land owned by Bishop Nixon, the state's first Anglican bishop. The Anglican Church built in 1844 still stands. Bishopsbourne is located 16km west of Longford. From Longford take the C519 road, or if travelling from the north take the C513 road from Carrick.

Bishopsbourne Recreational Ground

Signposted access to the recreational ground in Bishopsbourne. Designated area for fully self-contained caravans, motorhomes and campervans ie: units must have own fresh water storage, sealed grey water holding tank, sealed black water.

MR: Map 7 C1

FURTHER Information

> **Northern Midlands Council**
> **Tel:** 03 6397 7303
> **Web:** www.northernmidlands.tas.gov.au
> **Maximum stay:** 24 hours.

4 Branxholm

Situated on the B52 road, Branxholm is 25km east of Scottsdale and 8km west of Derby. Visit a hop farm or take a gemstone tour.

Branxholm camping ground

Situated beside the Ringarooma River, on the Tasman Highway in Branxholm Bring drinking water. Laundry facilities.
GPS S:41 10.096 E:147 44.221
MR: Map G6

FURTHER Information

Branxholm Shopping Centre
Tel: 03 6354 6168. Bookings recommended for powered sites during peak periods of December to April.
Camping fees: Unpowered from $7.00 per site/night. Powered from $14.00 per site/night. Key required for access and amenities, refundable key deposit required. Fees payable at Branxholm Shopping Centre in Scott Street.

5 Douglas—Apsley National Park

Situated north of Bicheno. Take the short walk to Apsley Waterhole or the 3-hour Apsley Gorge circuit. Those who prefer longer walks can walk the 3-day Leeaberra Track - this walk should be undertaken in a north to south direction. Access to the southern section is via Rosedale Road off the Tasman Highway, 4km north of Bicheno. Access to the northern section (and start of the 3-day walk) is via the gravel E Road off the Tasman Highway, 4km north of Bicheno.

Apsley Waterhole camping area

Located 11km north-west of Bicheno. Signposted access off Rosedale Road. Park at car park and walk 200m into campsite. Water available from river, boil first. Gas/fuel stove preferred.
MR: Map 8 I3

Heritage Falls & Tevelein Falls camping areas

Walk-in sites along the Leeaberra Track. Access start of walk from north of park. Self-sufficient bushwalkers. Bring drinking water. Gas/fuel stove only. Obtain large scale maps and contact ranger for further details.

FURTHER Information

Parks & Wildlife Service Freycinet
Tel: 03 6256 7000
Parks Pass: Required.
Fire Restrictions: Solid fuel fire ban between 1 October and April 30. Gas/fuel stove only during this period, unless days of total fire ban. Firewood collection in park is prohibited.
NB: To help reduce spread of Root Rot, please walk Leeaberra Track from north to south and clean boots and tent pegs before and after visiting.

6 Evandale

The historic village of Evandale is situated on the South Esk River. Home to a range of unspoiled heritage buildings, the village is a National Trust classified Georgian village. Every February Evandale holds the National Penny Farthing Championships, whilst the Evandale Markets are held every Sunday where local produce and crafts are on display. Evandale is accessed via the B41 highway and is 23km south of Launceston.

Falls Park

Located on Logan Road in Evandale. Signposted access. Designated area for fully self-contained caravans, motorhomes and campervans ie: units must have own fresh water storage, sealed grey water holding tank, sealed black water.

GPS S:41 34.267 E:147 15.233
MR: Map 3 E8

FURTHER Information

Northern Midlands Council
Tel: 03 6397 7303
Web: www.northernmidlands.tas.gov.au
Evandale Visitor Information Centre
Tel: 03 6391 8128
Web: www.evandaletasmania.com
Maximum stay: 24 hours. Overnight stops only available Monday to Friday nights.

7 Fingal

The mining village of Fingal is located to the west of St Marys on the A4 highway. Located in the village are a number of historic buildings.

Fingal Park camping area

Signposted access along the A4 highway in Fingal. Large grassed area for tent-based campers. Childrens playground. Power available. Sullage dump site.

GPS S:41 38.367 E:147 58.000
MR: Map 8 H1

FURTHER Information

Break O'Day Council
Tel: 03 6376 7900
Fingal Valley Neighbourhood Community House
Tel: 03 6374 2344
Maximum stay: 2 nights.

THE NORTH-EAST AND FLINDERS ISLAND

Flinders Island is the largest of the 70 islands that make up the Fureaux Group. The island has plenty to offer the nature lover, wildlife spotter and bushwalker. The Fureaux Group is one of the richest fishing areas in Australia. Access to the island is via air or sea. There is no public transport on the island, vehicles and bicycles can be hired.

Photo courtesy of Flinders Tourism Association/John de la Roche

Flinders Island Castle Rock

Yellow Beach Coastal Reserve camping area

Located 2km east of Lady Barron. From Lady Barron take the signposted Franklin Parade, and then take the signposted Pot Boil Road to the signposted beach access. Bring drinking water and firewood. Gas/fuel stove preferred.
MR: Map 9 D5

Allport Beach camping area

Sheltered campsite among trees opposite the beach, located 21km north of White-mark. Signposted access to Allport Beach is off Port Davies Road, south-west of Emita. Bring drinking water and firewood. Gas/fuel stove preferred.
MR: Map 9 B4

Lillies Beach camping area

Camping area on the beach. Access to Lillies Beach is signposted off Port Davies Road south-west of Emita. Good snorkelling area. Bring drinking water and firewood. Gas/fuel stove preferred.
MR: Map 9 B4

North East River camping area

Located 15km north-east of Killiecrankie. Numerous access tracks lead off the North East Road to campsites beside the river, 200m from the river mouth. Bring drinking water and firewood. NB: Be aware of undertows when swimming. Gas/fuel stove preferred.
MR: Map 9 C2

FURTHER Information

> **Flinders Island Visitor Information Centre**
> **Tel:** 1800 994 477
> **Web:** www.visitflindersisland.com.au

Photo courtesy of Flinders Tourism Association/Gary Sykes

North East River

GETTING TO Flinders Island

Vehicle-based campers can access Flinders Island via the freight and passenger vessels operated by Southern Shipping based at Bridport in the north-east of Tasmania. This service operates every Monday (unless a public holiday then on the Tuesday) from Bridport and returns from Flinders Island every Tuesday. Contact Southern Shipping on 03 6356 3333 or visit www.southernshipping.com.au

Access to Flinders Island is also possible via air with Airlines of Tasmania. Airlines of Tasmania operate daily services from Launceston and Essendon airports. Contact Airlines of Tasmania on 1800 144 460 or 03 6359 2312 or visit www.airtasmania.com.au

Once on Flinders Island there are vehicle and bicycle hire facilities available.

Granite Point Conservation Area is west of Bridport on Anderson Bay. The Bridport Caravan Park is within the conservation area and offers a beachside location. Access is signposted on Bentley Street in Bridport. Due to park layout, access for some larger vans could be tricky. Bridport is accessed off the B82 Road and is 58km east of George Town and 21km north of Scottsdale.

Bridport Caravan Park

Signposted access via Bentley Street in Bridport. Campsites situated in natural coastal vegetation. Gas BBQs for hire. Camp fires allowed, bring own fire pot and firewood. Laundry facilities.

GPS S:40 59.769 E:147 23.296

MR: Map 3 E5

FURTHER Information

Bridport Caravan Park

Tel: 03 6356 1227. Bookings recommended for Easter, Christmas and New Year.

Camping fees: Powered and unpowered sites available. Contact Bridport Caravan Park for current fees.

THE NORTH-EAST AND FLINDERS ISLAND

10 Humbug Point Nature Recreation Area

Large area situated on Georges Bay, with good access to the water. Access is signposted off Binalong Bay Road north of St Helens. The surrounding coastal vegetation and bay are visited by numerous bird species. This area is popular with bushwalkers and birdwatchers.

Moulting Bay camping area

Signposted access off Binalong Bay Road, 7km north of St Helens. Then drive in 900m to the well sheltered camping area. Suitable for big rigs. Beach boat launch. Bring drinking water and firewood. Gas/fuel stove preferred.

GPS S:41 16.880 E: 148 16.850
MR: Map 4 J7

Dora Point camping area

Signposted access off Binalong Bay Road, 8.2km north of St Helens, then 4.7km into camping area. Number of sheltered sites among coastal heath. Bring drinking water and firewood. Gas/fuel stove preferred.

GPS S:41 16.707 E:148 19.515
MR: Map 4 J7

FURTHER Information

> **Parks & Wildlife Service St Helens**
> **Tel:** 03 6376 1550
> **Parks Pass:** Not required.
> **Maximum stay:** 4 weeks.

11 Lagoons Beach Conservation Area

Situated east of St Marys and north of the A4, this coastal location offers visitors fishing and swimming opportunities.

Lagoons Beach camping area

Signposted access on the A3 highway. Access tracks are 1.9km and 2.3km north of the A3 and A4 junction. Spacious area behind beach stretching for 700m. Suitable for big rigs. Bring drinking water and firewood.

GPS S:41 39.034 E:148 17.713
MR: Map 8 J1

FURTHER Information

> **Parks & Wildlife Service Freycinet**
> **Tel:** 03 6256 7000
> **Parks Pass:** Not required.
> **NB:** Collection of firewood is prohibited in this area. Bring own firewood.

THE NORTH-EAST AND FLINDERS ISLAND

Access to this small, delightful reserve is signposted 2.4km north of Lilydale on the B81 highway. From the camping area there is a short walk to the falls. A children's playground is also located here.

Lilydale Falls camping area

Signposted access 2.4km north of Lilydale on the B81 highway. Vehicle-based stays are limited to car parking area. For tent-based campers, carry gear short distance to grassy sites. Some firewood supplied. Gas/fuel stove preferred.

GPS S:41 13.903 E:147 12.514

MR: Map 3 D6

FURTHER Information

Lilydale Newsagent & Take Away (Yummies)

Tel: 03 6395 1156

Maximum stay: 2 nights.

This historic and picturesque town is located west of the Midland Highway with access signposted off the highway, 20km south of Launceston. The town was established by free settlers in 1807, many of whom were provided with free convict labour. The toil of these convicts are still on show today with numerous convict-built houses about the town and surrounds.

Longford Riverside Caravan Park

Signposted access along Archer Street in Longford. Laundry facilities. Portable fireplaces are available from the office, with some firewood supplied.
GPS S:41 35.433 E:147 07.500
MR: Map 8 D1

FURTHER Information

Longford Riverside Caravan Park
Tel: 03 6391 1470
Camping fees: Unpowered from $25.00 per site/night for 2 people. Powered from $30.00 per site/night for 2 people.

THE NORTH-EAST AND FLINDERS ISLAND

Located in the far north-east of the region, Mt William National Park is home to a wonderful selection of beaches with fishing, diving and swimming opportunities, along with excellent wildlife viewing, beautiful coastal scenery and plenty of great bushwalks. See Forester Kangaroos grazing at dusk and dawn along the Forester Kangaroo Scenic Drive. The Eddystone Point Lighthouse is located in the south of the park and is accessed along the C846 road, which is signposted 3.4km west of Ansons Bay off the C843 road. The northern section of the park is accessed along the C845. To access the park from Gladstone take the C843 east for 8.1km, then take the C845 north for 8km to the park's information and self-registration booth. If travelling from the south, access can be had from St Helens by following the unsealed C843 north for 39.6km to the Ansons Bay Road, then turn west onto the C843 for 18.8km to the C845 road.

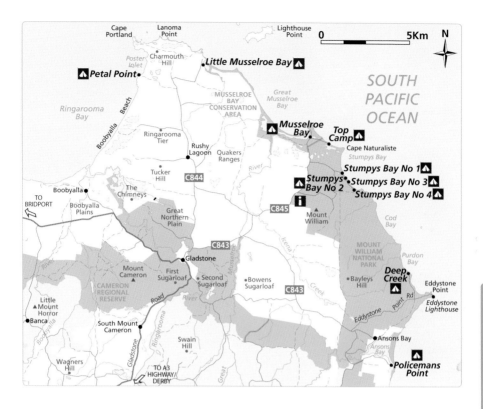

NORTHERN CAMPING AREAS

Top Camp campground

Signposted access along the C845, 7.9km north of the park information and self-registration booth. Then 2.3km east into open campsite with limited shade. Bring drinking water and firewood. Gas/fuel stove preferred.

GPS S:40 50.575 E:148 12.203
MR: Map 4 J4

Stumpys Bay: Campsite No 1

Signposted access 7.9km along the Forester Kangaroo Drive. The Forester Kangaroo Drive starts 1.1km north of the park information and self-registration booth. Access to campsite is signposted 800m east of the Forester Kangaroo Drive. Bring drinking water and firewood. Gas/fuel stove preferred.

GPS S:40 52.285 E:148 13.303
MR: Map 4 J4

Stumpys Bay: Campsite No 2

Signposted access 7.9km along the Forester Kangaroo Drive. Access track is signposted 400m past access track to Campsite No 1. This well-sheltered area is best suited for tent based camping. Bring drinking water. Gas/fuel stove only.

GPS S:40 52.598 E:148 13.581
MR: Map 4 J4

Stumpys Bay: Campsite No 3

Signposted access 7.9km along the Forester Kangaroo Drive. Access track is signposted 1km past access track to Campsite No 2. Suitable for small vans. Open sites, not as well shaded or protected as Campsite Nos 1 and 2. 4WD beach boat ramp. Bore water available, suitable for washing only. Bring drinking water and firewood. Gas/fuel stove preferred.

GPS S:40 52.758 E:148 13.753
MR: Map 4 J4

Stumpys Bay: Campsite No 4

Signposted access 7.9km along the Forester Kangaroo Drive. Access track is signposted 1.4km past access track to Campsite No 3. Open area with some protected sites. Shelter and gas BBQ in adjacent day use area. Bring drinking water. Gas/fuel stove only.

GPS S:40 53.276 E:148 14.244
MR: Map 4 J4

TOTAL Fire Bans

 On days that are declared a total fire ban it is illegal to light any fire in the open, in tents and in canvas camping trailers. This includes any naked flame (portable stoves, gas and solid fuel BBQ). It's your responsibility to be aware of which fire district your campsite falls under. Fire bans are usually broadcast on the local radio station.

Stumpys Bay Campsite No4

SOUTHERN CAMPING AREA

Deep Creek camping area

Signposted access 9.5km along the C846 (Eddystone Point Road), then drive 3.3km north to the campsite. The C846 (Eddystone Point Road) is signposted off the C843 road 3.4km west of Ansons Bay. Bring drinking water and firewood. Gas/fuel stove preferred.

GPS S:40 58.194 E:148 18.726
MR: Map 4 J4

FURTHER *Information*

Parks & Wildlife Service St Helens
Tel: 03 6376 1550
Parks Pass: Required.
Camping fees: From $13.00 per site/night up to 2 people. Fees payable at self-registration stations.

This popular birdwatching area is situated to the north and west of Mt William National Park. The north-western section of Musselroe Bay Conservation Area is accessed along the C844 (Cape Portland Road), whilst the eastern section, which is north of Mt William National Park, can be accessed from Gladstone by following the C843 and the C845 roads.

Little Musselroe Bay camping area

Located in the north-western part of the conservation area. Access is signposted 27.4km along the C844 (Cape Portland) road north of Gladstone. Then in 200m to the camping area with some sheltered sites on edge of the bay. Suitable for off-road camper trailers and caravans. Vehicle access only possible from Christmas to Easter. At other times site is walk-in only from the C844 road. Bring drinking water and firewood.

GPS S:40 45.982 E:148 02.018
MR: Map 4 I3

Musselroe Bay camping area

Located in the eastern section of the conservation area, 24km north-east of Gladstone and 100m north of the Mt William National Park Top Camp access road. Access is signposted along the C845 road, 7.9km north of Mt William National Park information and self-registration booth. Number of both open and sheltered campsites. Suitable for big rigs. Boat ramp nearby. Bring drinking water and firewood. Please use current fire sites, do not make new sites.

GPS S:40 50.155 E:148 10.659
MR: Map 4 J4

FURTHER Information

Parks & Wildlife Service St Helens
Tel: 03 6376 1550
Parks Pass: Not required.
Maximum stay: 4 weeks at Musselroe Bay camping area.

THE NORTH-EAST AND FLINDERS ISLAND

Located 40km east of Devonport, access to the park is signposted along the C740 road which is signposted off the B71 highway south-east of Devonport. Narawntapu National Park has a varied landscape of coastal inlets and beaches, sand dunes, wetlands and lagoons and the low ranges of Asbestos Range. These environments support a varied plant and animal life, with Forester kangaroos, Bennetts wallabies and common wombats seen grazing on the park's grasslands at dusk. Visitors to the park can enjoy bushwalking, safe beaches for swimming, water-skiing, and fishing as well as nature study and birdwatching, bike riding and horse riding. Please note that all bike riders are to stay to vehicle roads only, and conditions apply for horse riding. Check with park office for details.

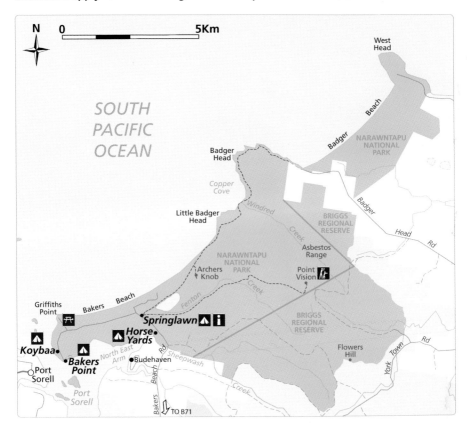

THE NORTH-EAST AND FLINDERS ISLAND

Bakers Point camping area, Narawntapu National Park

Horse Yards camping area

Signposted along park road, 600m in from park entrance. Limited drinking water. Some firewood supplied. Campers with horses must camp with horse and give notice 48 hours prior to arrival, conditions apply.

GPS S:41 09.224 E:146 36.588
MR: Map 3 A6

Koybaa camping area

Signposted access along main park road, 4km west of the Ranger Station. Tent based camping with 12 sites, carry gear over bollards. Walk to beach. Gas/fuel stove only. Bring drinking water.

GPS S:41 09.591 E:146 33.879
MR: Map 3 A6

Springlawn camping area

Signposted access along park road, 1km from park entrance and 100m past Ranger Station. Grassed area with 14 powered sites. Suitable for big rigs. Drinking water supplied, boil first. Token-operated hot showers, token from park office.

GPS S:41 08.907 E:146 36.127
MR: Map 3 A6

Springlawn camping area

Bakers Point camping area

Signposted access along park road, 4.5km west of Ranger Station. Large, scenic camping area along the foreshore with 36 sites, of which 16 are suitable for camper trailers, caravans and motorhomes. Most sites suitable for campervans. Boat ramp nearby. Portaloo waste collection station located here. Drinking water, boil first. Firewood supplied. Gas/fuel stove preferred.

GPS S:41 09.762 E:146 34.095
MR: Map 3 A6

FURTHER Information

> **Parks & Wildlife Service Narawntapu**
> **Tel:** 03 6428 6277
> **Parks Pass:** Required.
> **Camping fees:** From $13.00 per site/night up to 2 people. Powered sites at Springlawn CA from $16.00 per site/night for up to 2 people. Fees payable at self-registration station at Ranger Station.

17 Ringarooma Coastal Reserve

Situated on the north-east tip of the island on Ringarooma Bay. Access to the reserve is signposted off the Cape Portland Road from Gladstone. The campsite is situated at the northern end of Boobyalla Beach.

Petal Point camping area

Signposted access 21km along the C844 (Cape Portland Road) north of Gladstone, then 4.5km west into start of camping areas. Numerous tracks lead to campsites among vegetation and to open, exposed sites with great ocean views. Suitable for off-road camper trailers and caravans, as access road can be rough. Bring drinking water and firewood. Please use current fire sites, do not make new sites or carry own fire bin. Gas/fuel stove preferred.

GPS S:40 46.638 E:147 56.888
MR: Map 4 H3

FURTHER Information

> **Parks & Wildlife Service Scottsdale Field Centre**
> **Tel:** 03 6352 6421
> **Parks Pass:** Not required.

THE NORTH-EAST AND FLINDERS ISLAND

Saddleback Plantation is located to the west of Mathinna and home to the popular Griffin camping area. This large grassy area is situated beside the South Esk River, well known for trout fishing. Griffin camping area is located on the gravel Griffin Park Road which can be accessed off the C401 Road (west end) or the C423 road (east end).

Griffin camping area

Numerous access tracks signposted along Griffin Road, 2km, 3.5km and 5.2km west of the C423 road. Griffin Road is signposted off the C423 road 1.7km north of Mathinna. This camping area is a favourite site for trail bike riders, especially from December to Easter. Forest harvesting does occur in these regions, and the camping area may be closed at these times. Bring drinking water and firewood.

GPS S:41 27.966 E:147 51.087
MR: Map 4 G8

South Esk River picnic and camping area

Located at junction of C423 and Griffin Road, 1.7km north of Mathinna and the B43. Lovely grassed sites beside the South Esk River. Bring drinking water and firewood.

GPS S:41 27.826 E:147 53.428
MR: Map 4 H8

FURTHER Information

Forestry Tasmania Scottsdale
Tel: 03 6352 6466

THE NORTH-EAST AND FLINDERS ISLAND

Halls Falls near Pyengana

Situated to the south of St Helens the conservation area offers fishing, swimming, surfing and canoeing. Numerous campsites located on the eastern foreshore between basin and beach. Please note camping is only permitted at the designated camping area at Dianas Basin, not at St Helens Point.

Dianas Basin camping area

Signposted access off the A3 highway, 3.9km north of Beaumaris and 9km south of St Helens. Then drive in 500m to an access track on left which leads to open campsites, or drive a further 900m to area with numerous campsites protected in among the trees with shade. Bring drinking water and firewood.

Open area **GPS** S:41 22.543 E:148 17.267
Shaded area **GPS** S:41 22.223 E:148 17.574
MR: Map 4 J7

FURTHER Information

Parks & Wildlife Service St Helens
Tel: 03 6376 1550
Parks Pass: Not required.
Maximum stay: 4 weeks.

THE NORTH-EAST AND FLINDERS ISLAND

20 Scamander Conservation Area

Scamander Conservation Area stretches along the east coast from Falmouth in the south, north to Dianas Basin, protecting the coastal foreshore. The discovery of middens and tools provides evidence of a rich Aboriginal history.

Paddys Island camping area

Signposted access off the A3 highway, 2.5km north of Beaumaris. Small site behind vegetation beside road. Bring drinking water and firewood.
GPS S:41 23.718 E:148 17.346
MR: Map 4 J7

Shelly Point camping area

Signposted access off the A3 highway, 2.1km south of Beaumaris. Then 400m into sheltered camping area among vegetation close to road. Suitable for smaller caravans and campervans.
NB: Parking area near beach is day use only. Bring drinking water and firewood.
GPS S:41 26.068 E:148 16.427
MR: Map 4 J8

FURTHER Information

> **Parks & Wildlife Service St Helens**
> **Tel:** 03 6376 1550
> **Parks Pass:** Not required.
> **Maximum stay:** 4 weeks.

21 Scamander Forest Reserve

This forest reserve is situated north-west of Scamander and south-west of Beaumaris on the banks of Scamander River. Fish for bream or enjoy the quiet surrounds. Access from Beaumaris is via Skyline Drive which is signposted off the A3 highway at the tavern. Alternative access from Scamander is via the signposted C421 road. Have a good insect repellant packed in your gear.

Trout Creek camping area

Signposted access on Trout Creek Road. From Beaumaris take Skyline Drive for 700m, turn left into road signposted to Trout Creek. Follow this for 400m to next junction signposted to Trout Creek. Turn left, campsite is 3.3km along this road. From Scamander take the C421 road, which is signposted just south of Scamander, and follow it for 7km.

Turn right into signposted road to Trout Creek, follow this for 5.2km to junction signposted to Trout Creek. Turn right, campsite is 3.3km along this road. Shaded, grassed camping area beside the river. Bring drinking water and firewood.
GPS S:41 26.244 E:148 13.595
MR: Map 4 J8

FURTHER Information

> **Forestry Tasmania Scottsdale**
> **Tel:** 03 6352 6466

Trout Creek camping area, Scamander Forest Reserve

22 Scottsdale

Scottsdale is located on the A3 highway, 63km north-east of Launceston. Regarded as the hub of the north-east, it is surrounded by some of the state's richest forest and agricultural country. Visit the Forest EcoCentre. Beside the campground is a pleasant park and pond where ducks feed and maybe even a platypus could be spotted.

Northeast Park Campground

Signposted access on the A3 highway, 1km south-east of Scottsdale. Gas/fuel stove only.

GPS S:41 09.917 E:147 31.367
MR: Map 3 F6

FURTHER Information

Scottsdale Visitor Information Centre

Tel: 03 6352 6520
Web: www.northeasttasmania.com.au
Maximum stay: 7 nights.

Situated in the south-west corner of Flinders Island, Strzelecki National Park covers an area over 4200 hectares. The park has magnificent views of the surrounding islands and the coastline, and is home to tall granite peaks, beautiful wildflowers and local wildlife. Visitors can enjoy excellent swimming, fishing, diving and snorkelling. Access to the park is signposted along the B85 (Lady Barron Road) south of Whitemark. See page 33 for access information to Flinders Island.

Photo courtesy of Flinders Tourism Association/John de la Roche

Trousers Point camping area

Signposted access along the C806 road, 15km south of the Lady Barron Road. The C806 road is signposted off the Lady Barron Road south of Whitemark and north-west of Lady Barron. Some firewood supplied. Gas/fuel stove preferred.

MR: Map 9 C5

FURTHER Information

Parks & Wildlife Service Strzelecki National Park
Tel: 03 6359 2217
Parks Pass: Required.

THE NORTH-EAST AND FLINDERS ISLAND

Targa is on the A3 highway, 30km north-east of Launceston and 30km southwest of Scottsdale.

Myrtle Park Recreation Ground

Access signposted along the A3 highway, 30km south of Scottsdale. Lovely, large area with grassed, shady, sites beside the river. Some sites are open and unshaded. Suitable for big rigs. Bring drinking water. Some firewood supplied. Kiosk, playground, tennis court.

GPS S:41 18.633 E:147 21.850
MR: Map 3 E7

FURTHER Information

Caretaker

Tel: 03 6399 3368. Bookings recommended from November to end April.
Camping fees: From $6.00 per couple/family/night.

This large conservation area stretches from the coast inland to protect a range of vegetation including heathland and the permanent deep water lagoons of Blackmans Lagoon, Big Waterhouse and Little Waterhouse lakes. Waterhouse Conservation Area is home to diverse bird and wildlife, including a number of threatened birds and mammals, as well as the dwarf galaxias, a rare freshwater fish. There are two access roads into Waterhouse Conservation Area. Access to the south-western section and Blackmans Lagoon is signposted off the B82 (Waterhouse Road) 23km east of Bridport and 38km west of Gladstone. The other road, which accesses the majority of the recreation areas is Homestead Road, which is signposted off the B82, 26.3km east of Bridport and 35km west of Gladstone. All roads within Waterhouse Conservation Area are unsealed and not regularly maintained, these roads can be rough at times. It is recommended that conventional vehicles, campervans, caravans and motorhomes contact the Parks and Wildlife Field Centre to check conditions. Visitors to Waterhouse Conservation Area can utilize the 4WD beach boat launches, go fishing, boating and sailing, as well as bird and wildlife spotting.

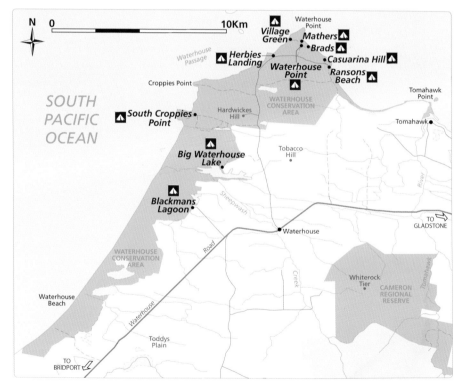

THE NORTH-EAST AND FLINDERS ISLAND

Blackmans Lagoon camping area

Signposted access along the B82 (Waterhouse Road), 23km east of Bridport and 3.3km west of Homestead Road. Then drive in 2.6km to camping area at southern end of the lagoon among pine trees. Camp only in signposted area.

Best suited for camper trailers, caravans, motorhomes and campervans. Boat ramp nearby. 4WD beach access for surf fishing from campsite. Bring drinking water and firewood. Gas/fuel stove preferred.

GPS S:40 54.769 E:147 35.714
MR: Map 3 F4

Big Waterhouse Lake camping area

Signposted access 4.3km along Homestead Road, then drive in a westerly direction for 2.6km to the camping area with a few cleared sites among the vegetation on the northern shore of the lake. Homestead Road is signposted off the B82 (Waterhouse Road), 26.3km east of Bridport and 35km west of Gladstone. Bring drinking water and firewood. Gas/fuel stove preferred.

GPS S:40 53.524 E:147 36.948
MR: Map 4 G4

Shack near Big Waterhouse Lake

South Croppies Point camping area

Signposted access along Homestead Road, 2km north of Big Waterhouse Lake access track. Then drive in a westerly direction for 1.7km to Y-junction. There are a number of cleared bush campsites along the track to the left and track to the right at this junction. Recommended to bring own portable toilet. Bring drinking water and firewood. Gas/fuel stove preferred.

GPS S:40 51.959 E:147 35.726
MR: Map 4 G4

Herbies Landing camping area

Signposted access along Homestead Road, 4.6km north of South Croppies Point access track. Small area close to the road suitable for three sites. Beach boat launch. Recommended to bring own portable toilet. Bring drinking water and firewood. Gas/fuel stove preferred.

GPS S:40 50.111 E:147 39.005
MR: Map 4 G4

Waterhouse Point camping area

Signposted access along Homestead Road, 1.4km east of Herbies Landing access track. Then drive north for 700m to track junction. Dispersed bush camping is available in this vicinity and along the access track to the east. Bring drinking water and firewood. Gas/fuel stove preferred.

GPS S:40 49.826 E:147 40.412
MR: Map 4 G3

Brads camping area

Accessed via the signposted access track to Waterhouse Point, which is 1.4km east of Herbies Landing. At the junction 700m north of Homestead Road, turn right and drive in an easterly direction for 400m to the camping area. Beach boat launch. Bring drinking water and firewood. Gas/fuel stove preferred.

GPS S:40 49.826 E:147 40.412
MR: Map 4 G3

Village Green camping area

Accessed via the signposted access track to Waterhouse Point, which is 1.4km east of Herbies Landing. At the junction 700m north of Homestead Road, turn left and drive in a westerly direction for 800m to the open, grassed camping area with limited shade. Beach boat launch. Bring drinking water and firewood. Gas/fuel stove preferred.

GPS S:40 49.613 E:147 39.685
MR: Map 4 G3

Mathers camping area

Accessed via the signposted access track to Waterhouse Point, which is 1.4km east of Herbies Landing. At the junction 700m north of Homestead Road, continue straight ahead in a northerly direction for 100m to the small camping area among coastal vegetation with some shaded and protected sites. Beach boat launch. Bring drinking water and firewood. Gas/fuel stove preferred.

GPS S:40 49.662 E:147 40.141
MR: Map 4 G3

Ransons Beach

Casuarina Hill camping area

Signposted access along Homestead Road, 1.7km east of Waterhouse Point access track. Then drive in a northerly direction for 400m to the small protected camping area. Access track is steep and rutted. Bring drinking water and firewood. Gas/fuel stove preferred.

GPS S:40 50.208 E:147 41.107
MR: Map 4 G3

Ransons Beach camping area

Accessed along Homestead Road 200m east of the Casuarina Hill access track. Small area suitable for one or two tent sites, close to private shacks. Beach boat launch. 4WD beach access seasonally closed from December 1 to weekend after Easter. Recommended to bring own portable toilet. Bring drinking water and firewood. Gas/fuel stove preferred.

GPS S:40 50.424 E:147 41.282
MR: Map 4 G3

FURTHER *Information*

Parks & Wildlife Service Scottsdale Field Centre
Tel: 03 6352 6421
Parks Pass: Not required.
Maximum stay: 4 weeks.
NB: Beach driving is possible in the designated areas and/or the launching and retrieval of boats, contact Parks and Wildlife Service Scottsdale Field Centre for details.

Located on the A3 highway, 42km north-west of St Helens. Weldborough has a colourful past. Popular gem fossicking area nearby.

Weldborough Hotel camping ground

Located on the Tasman Highway in Weldborough, 21km south-east of Derby and 42km north-west of St Helens. Shady grassed area behind the historic Weldborough Hotel. Bring drinking water, firewood and own fire pot/bin.

GPS S:41 11.659 E:147 54.285
MR: Map 4 H6

FURTHER Information

Weldborough Hotel
Tel: 03 6354 2223
Web: www.weldborough.com.au
Camping fees: From $5.00 per person/night. Power available, surcharge applicable.

THE NORTH-EAST AND FLINDERS ISLAND

Westbury is located along the Meander Valley Road (Old Bass Highway) 16km east of Deloraine and 35km west of Launceston. Andy's Bakery Cafe offers camping behind the bakery. The bakery is open 24 hours.

Andy's Motorhome and Camper Park

Located behind cafe at 45 Meander Valley Road. Coin-operated showers. Bakery cafe open 24 hours. Wireless internet access. Sullage dump.

GPS S:41 31.567 E:146 50.733
MR: Map 3 C8

FURTHER Information

Andy's Bakery Cafe
Tel: 03 6393 1846
Web: www.andystasmania.com
Camping fees: From $6.00 per person/ night.

Tree carvings at Legerwood

THE NORTH-EAST AND FLINDERS ISLAND

The South-East and Bruny Island

STRETCHING TO THE NORTH AND south of Hobart, the state's capital city, Tasmania's scenic South-East is a haven for water-based activities with opportunities to explore delightful destinations such as Bruny Island, the Tasman Peninsula and the stunning Freycinet National Park.

BEST Campsites!

 Richardsons Beach tent-based camping area
Freycinet National Park

 Fortescue Bay Campground
Tasman National Park

 Cloudy Bay Corner Beach campground
South Bruny National Park

 Lime Bay camping area
Lime Bay State Reserve

 Mayfield Bay camping area
Mayfield Bay Conservation Area

Separated from the mainland by D'Entrecasteaux Channel, Bruny Island, which is accessed via a vehicular ferry service from Kettering, offers a number of camping areas as well as a range of other activities, including boating, which is popular here.

Lying to the east of Hobart is the Tasman Peninsula, the site of convict-built Port Arthur settlement as well as historic Lime Bay State Reserve, also a reminder of convict times. Tasman National Park, which takes in the south-east corner of the peninsula has vehicle-based and walk-in camping areas.

In the north is one of the region's more popular parks, Freycinet National Park. This spectacular park is well visited during the summer months and has a range of camping areas which are ideal to base yourself while exploring the park via its many walking trails. One walk not to be missed in the park is to the picturesque Wineglass Bay. Also in this area is Maria Island, located offshore from Orford and reached via a ferry from Triabunna. It was at one time a penal settlement but is now a national park offering camping.

Spring, summer and autumn are without doubt the best times to experience this region.

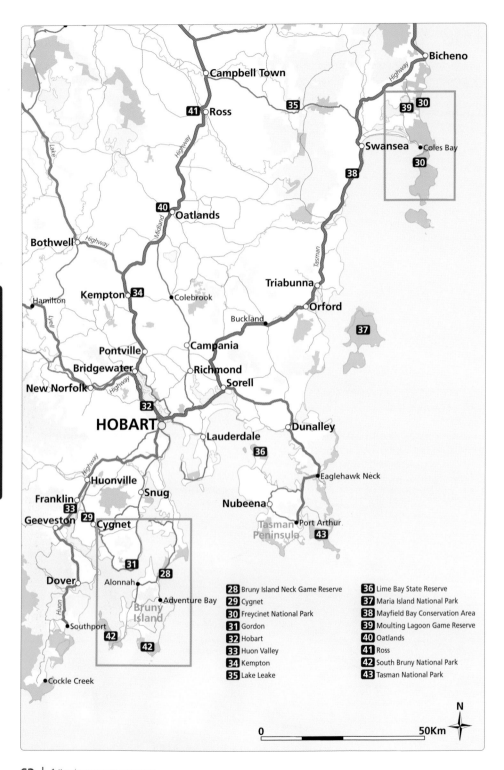

28 Bruny Island Neck Game Reserve	**36** Lime Bay State Reserve
29 Cygnet	**37** Maria Island National Park
30 Freycinet National Park	**38** Mayfield Bay Conservation Area
31 Gordon	**39** Moulting Lagoon Game Reserve
32 Hobart	**40** Oatlands
33 Huon Valley	**41** Ross
34 Kempton	**42** South Bruny National Park
35 Lake Leake	**43** Tasman National Park

N

0   50Km

Bruny Island Neck Game Reserve is located just to the south of the neck which joins North and South Bruny Islands. Signposted access off the B66 road leads to the campsite behind the beach. Limited caravan access. Access to the island is via the ferry service from Kettering.

The Neck camping area

Located on Lutregala Road. Signposted access off the B66 main road, 27.1km south of the ferry terminal and 3.2km north of the B66 and C630 junction. Bring drinking water and firewood.

GPS S:43 17.583 E:147 19.620
MR: Map 11 E5

FURTHER Information

Parks & Wildlife Service
Bruny Island
Tel: 03 6293 1419
Parks & Wildlife Service Huonville
Tel: 03 6264 8460
Parks Pass: Not required.
Camping fees: From $10.00 per site/night up to 2 people.

Originally named Port de Cygnet Noir (Black Swanport) due to the number of swans in the bay, today Cygnet is a fruit and wine growing area. Located in the heart of the village, the holiday park is a convenient location from where you can take a stroll along one of the area's beaches, visit The Tahune Devil Park or take a drive to Pelverata Falls. Cygnet is on the B68 road, 18km south of Huonville.

Cygnet Holiday Park

Located on Mary Street in Cygnet behind the RSL club and in front of the recreation ground. Access is signposted off the highway. Camp kitchen, laundry.

GPS S:43 09.371 E:147 04.486
MR: Map 11 D4

FURTHER Information

Cygnet Holiday Park
Tel: 0418 532 160 or 0400 682 099
Camping fees: Unpowered from $8.50 per person/night. Powered from $25.00 per site/ night for 2 people.

THE SOUTH-EAST AND BRUNY ISLAND

Freycinet National Park is one of Tasmania's most popular coastal destinations. The park offers visitors a range of recreational activities including swimming, snorkelling, beach fishing, scenic drives and a variety of walking tracks to explore. There is magnificent scenery of mountain ranges and beautiful white sandy beaches with clear blue waters. Access to the park is via the Coles Bay Road (C302) off the A3 highway, 11km south of Bicheno. The park's visitor information centre is 1.4km south of Coles Bay.

Richardsons Beach campervan & caravan campground

Access is 300m north of the park visitor information centre along Freycinet Drive. Camping area for camper trailers, caravans, motorhomes and campervans. 18 powered sites. Gas/fuel stove only.

GPS S:42 07.446 E:148 17.781
MR: Map 8 J5

Richardsons Beach tent-based camping area

Access on Freycinet Drive just south of the park visitor information centre. Tent-based camping only. Gas/fuel stove only.

GPS S:42 07.583 E:148 17.965
MR: Map 8 J5

Honeymoon Bay camping area

Signposted access on Freycinet Drive, 1.6km south of the park visitor information centre. Tent-based camping only. Gas/fuel stove only. Open Summer and Easter only.

GPS S:42 08.228 E:148 17.948
MR: Map 8 J5

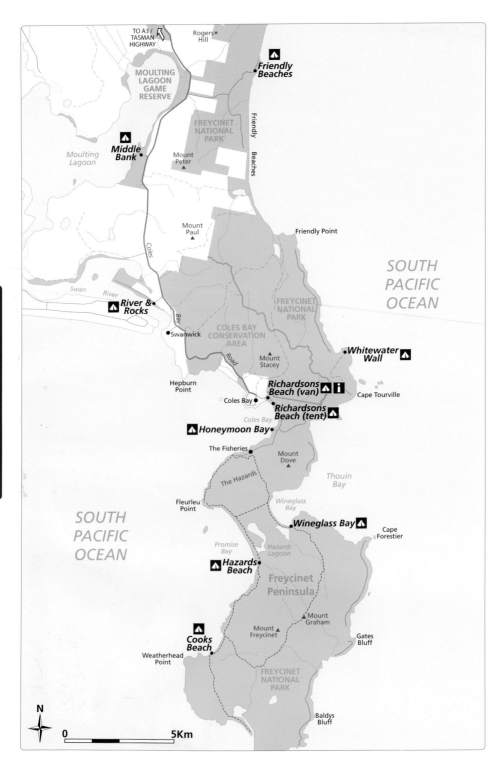

TO A3 /
TASMAN
HIGHWAY

Rogers
Hill

**Friendly
Beaches**

MOULTING
LAGOON
GAME
RESERVE

FREYCINET
NATIONAL
PARK

Friendly

Moulting
Lagoon

**Middle
Bank**

Mount
Peter

Beaches

Mount
Paul

Friendly Point

SOUTH
PACIFIC
OCEAN

Coles

Swan

River

**River &
Rocks**

FREYCINET
NATIONAL
PARK

Bay

Swanwick

COLES BAY
CONSERVATION
AREA

Road

Mount
Stacey

**Whitewater
Wall**

Hepburn
Point

**Richardsons
Beach (van)**

Cape Tourville

Coles Bay

**Richardsons
Beach (tent)**

Coles Bay

Honeymoon Bay

The Fisheries

Mount
Dove

Thouin
Bay

The Hazards

Fleurieu
Point

Wineglass
Bay

Wineglass Bay

Cape
Forestier

SOUTH
PACIFIC
OCEAN

Promise
Bay

Hazards
Lagoon

**Hazards
Beach**

Freycinet
Peninsula

Mount
Graham

Mount
Freycinet

Gates
Bluff

**Cooks
Beach**

Weatherhead
Point

FREYCINET
NATIONAL
PARK

N

0   5Km

Baldys
Bluff

Friendly Beaches camping area

Signposted access along the Coles Bay Road (C302), 8.6km south of the A3 highway. Then 3.9km east into camping area along unsealed road. Individual sites among coastal vegetation above beach. Limited sites suitable for campervans. Bring drinking water. Gas/fuel stove only.

GPS S:41 59.488 E:148 17.205
MR: Map 8 J4

Whitewater Wall camping area

Access track is 2.1km along Cape Tourville Road, which is 1.6km south of the park visitor information centre. Then 2.1km into the small sheltered camping area. Gas/fuel stove only.

GPS S:42 06.297 E:148 20.309
MR: Map 8 J4

Walk-in campsites: Wineglass Bay, Hazards Beach and Cooks Beach

Walk-in bush campsites within the park for overnight self-sufficient walkers. Carry large scale maps. Gas/fuel stove only. Contact Ranger for details of water availability. Walkers must register and deregister at the information/self-registration station in the main car park.

FURTHER Information

Parks & Wildlife Service Freycinet Visitors Centre

Tel: 03 6256 7000. Ballot system for Christmas holiday period applies, entries in by July 31. Campground bookings are taken for December 19 to February 10 and for Easter only. Outside of these times fees payable at visitor information centre or self-registration stations.
Parks Pass: Required.
Camping fees: Richardsons Beach campervan and caravan campground – all sites are powered: From $16.00 per site/night for 2 people. Richardsons Beach tent based and Honeymoon Bay camping areas: From $13.00 per site/night for 2 people.

Friendly Beaches camping area

31 Gordon

Gordon is a small locality on the waters of the D'Entrecasteaux Channel. Access to Gordon is along the B68 road, which is signposted off the A6 highway at Kingston, 11km south of Hobart or from Huonville, 35km south-west of Hobart.

Gordon Oval Reserve

Located on Channel Highway in Gordon. Overnight camping area at the Gordon Oval, camp only in the designated area. Located close to the Gordon Jetty where the boat ramp is located. Bring drinking water.

MR: Map 11 E4

FURTHER Information

Kingborough Council
Tel: 03 6211 8200
Web: www.kingborough.tas.gov.au
Camping fees: From $5.00 per site/night. Payable at on-site honesty box.
Maximum stay: 24 hours.

32 Hobart

The state's capital city is situated on the Derwent River at the foot of the majestic Mount Wellington. This historic harbour city offers a range of activities for the visitor. Visit Risdon Cove; Salamanca Place; Constitution Dock; the Cascade Brewery, museums and art galleries; view historic buildings (there's over ninety buildings in Hobart classified by the National Trust); take a cruise along the river or join a tour of the Cadbury chocolate factory.

Hobart Showground Motorhome Park

Signposted access on Howard Road, which is signposted off the Brooker Highway in Glenorchy, north of Hobart city centre. Camping approved for fully self-contained caravans, motorhomes and campervans ie: units must have own fresh water storage, sealed grey water holding tank, sealed black water holding tank. Camping permit issued from administration office on arrival or at self-registration station outside business hours.

GPS S:42 50.033 E:147 17.100
MR: Map 11 E2

FURTHER Information

Royal Hobart Showground
Tel: 03 6272 6812
Web: www.hobartshowground.com.au
Camping fees: Unpowered site from $20.00 per site/night. Powered site from $25.00 per site/night.
Maximum stay: 14 nights. No camping available during October.

THE SOUTH-EAST AND BRUNY ISLAND

Cascade Brewery, Hobart

33 Huon Valley

Located to the south-west of Hobart, the area is renowned for fresh produce including apples and seafood as well as locally made wines. Nature lovers will enjoy the pristine rivers, caves and beautiful national parks. The Huon Valley Council provides camping and caravan areas in the towns of Franklin and Port Huon.

Franklin Foreshore camping & caravan area

Signposted access on the A6 highway in Franklin. No open fires on ground, bring own fire drum/pot and firewood. Camping permit issued when fees are collected.

GPS S:43 05.499 E:147 00.592
MR: Map 11 C3

FURTHER Information

Huon Valley Council
Tel: 03 6264 0300
Web: www.huonvalley.tas.gov.au
Camping fees: From $10.00 per site/night. Fees collected daily.
Maximum stay: 4 nights.

Franklin Foreshore camping and caravan area, Huon Valley

Shipwrights Point Regatta Ground/Recreation Reserve

Signposted access on the A6 highway at northern end of Port Huon. Camping permit issued when fees are collected.

GPS S:43 09.5100 E:146 58.759
MR: Map C4

FURTHER Information

Huon Valley Council
Tel: 03 6264 0300
Web: www.huonvalley.tas.gov.au
Camping fees: From $10.00 per site/night. Fees collected daily.
Maximum stay: 4 nights.

Shipwrights Point Regatta Ground/Recreation Reserve

CAMPING with your dog

 If you own a well behaved and well socialised dog you may wish to take your 'best friend' along camping with you. Dogs are usually welcome in state forests and some reserves, but are not permitted in national parks. Each listing in this guide indicates whether you can bring your dog with you.

34 Kempton

The village of Kempton is located on the Midland Highway, approximately 50km north of Hobart. The town has many historical buildings.

Kempton overnight bay

Located behind 'The Blue Place' on Main Street in Kempton. Access road is diagonally opposite council chambers.

GPS S:42 31.917 E:147 12.133
MR: Map 7 D7

FURTHER Information

Southern Midlands Council
Tel: 03 6259 3011
Camping fee: From $10.00 per vehicle/night, or free for self-contained units that do not use facilities. Refundable key deposit required for facilities key. There is an on-site donation box for the local Green Ponds Progress Association who maintain the site. Collect facilities key and pay fees to Southern Midlands Council, Main Street Kempton during week days between 8.30am and 4.30pm.
Maximum stay: 1 night.
Gray water dump station located at rear of Victoria Hall in town.

35 Lake Leake

Lake Leake is located 4km north of the B34 Road between Campbell Town and Swansea. It's a popular spot with anglers chasing trout.

Lake Leake camping area

Located 3.6km north of the B34 highway. Access is signposted off the B34, 28.5km west of the A3 highway and 34km east of Campbell Town. Unsealed access road. Small area. Bring drinking water and firewood.

GPS S:42 00.526 E:147 47.854
MR: Map 8 G4

FURTHER Information

Lake Leake Caretaker
Tel: 03 6381 1319
Camping fees: Unpowered from $10.00 per site/night for 2 people. Powered from $20.00 per site/night for 2 people. Additional people from $2.00 per person/night.
NB: There are no credit card or Eftpos facilities, cash only payments.

THE SOUTH-EAST AND BRUNY ISLAND

36 Lime Bay State Reserve

The reserve is situated on the Tasman Peninsula north of Premaydena. Colourful wildflowers are abundant during summer and the beaches at Lime Bay offer enjoyable walking. Visit the ruins of the convict station at nearby Coal Mines Historic Site. Access is signposted from Premaydena, which is 9.3km west of Taranna via the B37 off the Arthur Highway (A9).

Lime Bay camping area

Located 18km north of Premaydena at the end of the Coal Mines Road. From Premaydena follow the C341 signposted to Coal Mines Historic Site which is 11.9km north-west of Premaydena. Continue past the historic site for a further 6.6km to the shaded camping area on the waterfront. Suitable for big rigs. Bring drinking water and firewood. Gas/fuel stove preferred.

GPS S:42 57.419 E:147 42.259
MR: Map 12 G2

FURTHER Information

Parks & Wildlife Service Seven Mile Beach
Tel: 03 6214 8100
Parks Pass: Not required.
Camping fees: From $13.00 per site/night for 2 people. Fees payable at on-site self-registration station.

THE SOUTH-EAST AND BRUNY ISLAND

Maria Island was named by Abel Tasman in 1642, in honour of Maria Van Diemen, the wife of the governor of Batavia. The island's history includes a long-time association with local Aboriginal tribes who once canoed across to the island, and with European settlement when the island became a penal settlement in the early 1820s. Escaping convicts would swim or use rafts to return to mainland Tasmania. The penal settlement was abandoned around 1832 and the island's convicts were then housed at Port Arthur. Nowadays, visitors can visit the historic ruins of the convict days and discover the island's past agricultural pursuits. Take in the beautiful bays, rugged cliffs, enjoy one of the many walking tracks, take a bike ride along the island's roads and view an array of birds and wildlife. Access to Maria Island is via a 30-minute ferry trip from Triabunna wharf. Triabunna is signposted along the Tasman Highway (A3 road), 57km north of Sorell and 50km south of Swansea.

Triabunna

Darlington camping area

Located in Darlington, 200 metres from ferry jetty. Coin-operated hot showers. Laundry facilities. Some firewood supplied. Gas/fuel stove preferred.

MR: Map 8 I8

Frenchs Farm camping area

Located 11km south of Darlington. Access is signposted. Gas/fuel stove only.

MR: Map 8 I8

THE SOUTH-EAST AND BRUNY ISLAND

Encampment Cove camping area

Located 13km south of Darlington.
Access is signposted. Firewood supplied.
Gas/fuel stove preferred.

MR: Map 8 I8

FURTHER Information

Parks & Wildlife Service Maria Island
Tel: 03 6257 1420
Parks Pass: Required.
Camping fees: From $13.00 per site/night for 2 people. Fees payable at Commissariat Store. Other accommodation available at the Penitentiary Units, contact office for bookings and fees.
Ferry service: Maria Island Ferry & Eco Cruises
Tel: 0419 746 668. Reservations essential.
Web: www.mariaislandferry.com.au

38 Mayfield Bay Conservation Area

Mayfield Bay Conservation Area is signposted along the Tasman Highway, 15km south of Swansea and 13km north of Little Swanport. The beaches at Mayfield Bay offer diving, swimming and fishing. Take the short walk to Three Arch Bridge, built in 1845 by convicts.

Mayfield Bay camping area

Signposted access on the Tasman Highway (A3), 15km south of Swansea. Beach boat launch. Bring drinking water and firewood.

GPS S:42 14.406 E:148 00.758
MR: Map 8 I5

FURTHER Information

Parks & Wildlife Service Freycinet
Tel: 03 6256 7000
Parks Pass: Not required.
Camping fees: Donation, payable at on-site donation box.
NB: Wood collection is not permitted in this area.

THE SOUTH-EAST AND BRUNY ISLAND

Game reserve on shores of Moulting Lagoon. Access is along the Coles Bay Road, south of the Freycinet National Park Friendly Beaches access road.

Middle Bank camping area

Access track is off Coles Bay Road, 3.6km south of the Friendly Beaches Road. Then 200m west into the small camping area, best suited for tent-based camping and self-sufficient campers. Recommended to bring own portable toilet. Bring drinking water and firewood. **NB:** Pets are not permitted at this site.

GPS S:42 01.563 E:148 13.453
MR: Map 8 J4

River and Rocks camping area

Signposted access off Coles Bay Road, 6.9km south of the Middle Bank access track and 7.4km north of Coles Bay. Then 400m west into the well-shaded and popular camping area. Bring drinking water and firewood. **NB:** Dog regulations may change in the future.

GPS S:42 05.198 E:148 13.910
MR: Map 8 J4

FURTHER Information

Parks & Wildlife Service Freycinet
Tel: 03 6256 7000
Parks Pass: Not required.

River and Rocks camping area

THE SOUTH-EAST AND BRUNY ISLAND

40 Oatlands

The village of Oatlands is located on the Midland Highway, 86km south of Ross and 90km north of Hobart. Numerous historic buildings, antique stores, cafes and a Historical Centre. A walk around the lake is accessible to wheelchairs.

Lake Dulverton camping area

Signposted access along The Esplande in Oatlands. Public phone nearby in town.

GPS S:42 18.050 E:147 22.567
MR: Map 7 E6

FURTHER Information

The Central Tasmanian Tourism Centre, 'The Stables' 85 High Street Oatlands
Tel: 03 6254 1212
Maximum stay: 3 nights.

41 Ross

The picturesque village of Ross is accessed off the Midland Highway. The town's historic buildings date back to the early and mid 1800s. The locally produced information guide has details of these buildings and other attractions, see the Visitor Information Centre on arrival.

Ross Caravan Park

Located at the end of The Esplande beside the Ross Motel and adjacent to the Macquarie River. Signposted access. Laundry facilities. Located close to town, walk to all town attractions and facilities.

GPS S:42 01.795 E:147 29.454
MR: Map 7 F4

FURTHER Information

Ross Motel
Tel: 03 6381 5224
Web: www.rossmotel.com.au
Camping fees: Unpowered from $24.00 per site/night for 2 people. Powered from $30.00 per site/night for 2 people.

THE SOUTH-EAST AND BRUNY ISLAND

South Bruny National Park

Situated at the southern tip of South Bruny Island, the park covers coastline areas with magnificent scenery, abundant wildlife and some rare vegetation. Access to the island is via the vehicular ferry from Kettering.

Jetty Beach camping area

Signposted access 17km south of Lunawanna along Cape Bruny Road (C629). Then drive in 2.3km to the camping area with dispersed sites among coastal vegetation. Access track is a narrow, single lane track. Beach boat launch. Bring drinking water and firewood. Gas/fuel stove preferred.

GPS S:43 27.580 E:147 09.157
MR: Map 11 D6

The Pines camping area

Signposted access 9km south of Lunawanna along Cloudy Bay Road (C644). Then drive in 600m to the small camping area in grove of pines. Bring drinking water and firewood. Gas/fuel stove preferred.

GPS S:43 26.246 E:147 14.807
MR: Map 11 E6

THE SOUTH-EAST AND BRUNY ISLAND

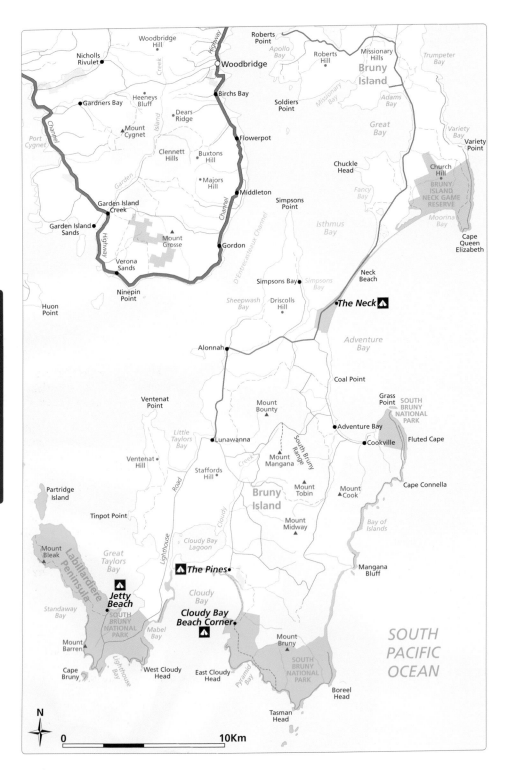

Nicholls
Rivulet

Woodbridge
Hill

Roberts
Point

Apollo
Bay

Roberts
Hill

Missionary
Hills

Trumpeter
Bay

Woodbridge

Bruny
Island

Gardners Bay

Heeneys
Bluff

Birchs Bay

Soldiers
Point

Adams
Bay

Dears
Ridge

Mount
Cygnet

Flowerpot

Great
Bay

Missionary
Bay

Variety
Bay

Variety
Point

Port
Cygnet

Clennett
Hills

Buxtons
Hill

Chuckle
Head

Church
Hill

BRUNY
ISLAND
NECK GAME
RESERVE

Garden
Island

Majors
Hill

Middleton

Fancy
Bay

Moorina
Bay

Garden Island
Creek

Simpsons
Point

Isthmus
Bay

Cape
Queen
Elizabeth

Garden Island
Sands

Mount
Grosse

Gordon

Verona
Sands

D'Entrecasteaux Channel

Neck
Beach

Ninepin
Point

Simpsons Bay

Simpsons
Bay

●The Neck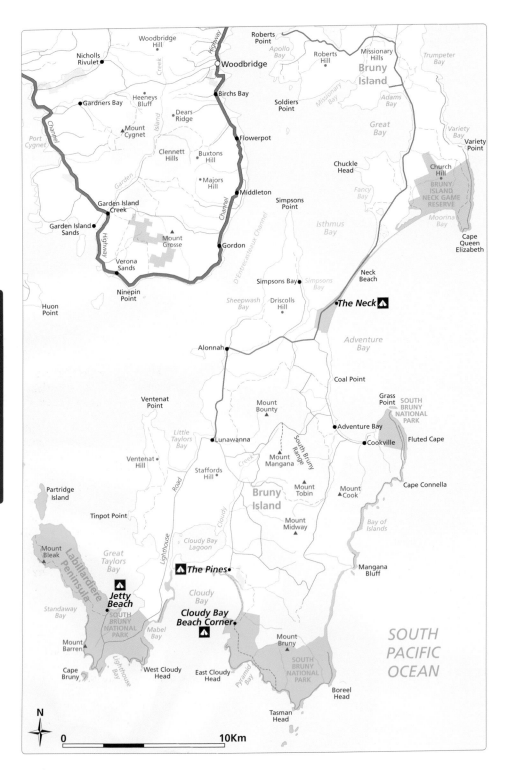

Huon
Point

Sheepwash
Bay

Driscolls
Hill

Alonnah

Adventure
Bay

Ventenat
Point

Mount
Bounty

Coal Point

Grass
Point

SOUTH
BRUNY
NATIONAL
PARK

Little
Taylors
Bay

Lunawanna

Adventure Bay

Fluted Cape

Ventenat
Hill

Staffords
Hill

Mount
Mangana

South Bruny Range

Cookville

Cape Connella

Partridge
Island

Creek

Bruny
Island

Mount
Tobin

Mount
Cook

Tinpot Point

Labillardiere Peninsula

Cloudy

Mount
Midway

Bay of
Islands

Mount
Bleak

Great
Taylors
Bay

Cloudy Bay
Lagoon

Lighthouse Road

🏕The Pines●

Mangana
Bluff

Standaway
Bay

🏕
Jetty
Beach

SOUTH
BRUNY
NATIONAL
PARK

Cloudy
Bay

Cloudy Bay
Beach Corner
🏕

SOUTH
PACIFIC
OCEAN

Mount
Barren

Mabel
Bay

Lighthouse Bay

West Cloudy
Head

East Cloudy
Head

Mount
Bruny

SOUTH
BRUNY
NATIONAL
PARK

Cape
Bruny

Pyramid Bay

Boreel
Head

Tasman
Head

N

0   10Km

Cloudy Bay Corner Beach campground

4WD beach access, 9.9km south of Lunawanna at end of Cloudy Bay Road (C644). Camping area is located 3km from beach entrance track via Cloudy Bay Beach. Check tide times prior to driving on the beach. Unpatrolled beach, be aware of rips when swimming. Popular surfing beach. Beach boat launch. Bring drinking water and firewood. Gas/fuel stove preferred.

GPS S:43 28.090 E:147 14.967
MR: Map 11 E6

FURTHER Information

Parks & Wildlife Service Bruny Island
Tel: 03 6293 1419
Parks & Wildlife Service Huonville
Tel: 03 6264 8460
Parks Pass: Required.
Camping fees: From $10.00 per site/night for 2 people

43 Tasman National Park

Along with the beautiful coastal scenery, Tasman National Park also offers visitors bushwalking, swimming and fishing opportunities. Signposted access to the park's campground at Fortescue Bay is off the Arthur Highway (A9). Access the north of the park via the Blowhole Road (C338).

TASMAN NATIONAL PARK WALK-IN CAMPSITES

Bivouac Bay campsite

Walk-in bush campsite along the Tasman Trail, north of Fortescue Bay. Trail can be accessed from Fortescue Bay Campground or from the north from Waterfall Bay Road. Gas/fuel stove only. Carry drinking water and maps.

MR: Map 12 H3

Camp Falls campsite

Walk-in bush campsite along the Tasman Trail, south of Waterfall Bay carpark. Trail can be accessed from Waterfall Bay Road or from the south from Fortescue Bay Campground. Gas/fuel stove only. Carry drinking water and maps.

MR: Map 12 H3

FURTHER Information

Parks & Wildlife Service Taranna
Tel: 03 6250 3497
Fortescue Bay Campground
Tel: 03 6250 2433
Parks Pass: Required.

Fortescue Bay Campground

Signposted access along the A9 highway, 3.4km south of the A9/B37 junction and 4km north of Port Arthur. Then drive in south-easterly direction for 12.2km to large camping area situated around the bay with 41 sites. Limited sites for big rigs. Hot showers operated by tokens, available for purchase from office. Boil drinking water. Bring firewood or purchase on site.

GPS S:43 08.512 E:147 57.810
MR: Map 12 H4

FURTHER Information

Fortescue Bay Campground
Tel: 03 6250 2433. Bookings necessary.
Parks Pass: Required.
Camping fees: From $13.00 per site/night for 2 people. Fees payable to caretaker at Fortescue Bay office.

The South-West Wilderness

THE SOUTH-WEST IS A VAST TRACT OF rugged and spectacular wilderness with few roads, although a number of camping opportunities exist at some picturesque locations around the fringe of this huge forested area. Much of this region is protected by the Southwest National Park, which has a selection of vehicle-based campsites and is also traversed by a number of multi-day walking trails. The famed lakes of Pedder and Gordon sit in the centre of the region and are surrounded by the park. A haven for anglers and bushwalkers, access to this World Heritage area is via Westerway. En route visitors can enjoy the nearby Mt Field National Park, which along with delightful Russell Falls also offers a number of walking trails as well the popular Land of Giants camping area.

Well-visited locations in the southern part of the region are around Recherche Bay where there are some delightful camping areas bordering the Southwest National Park at Cockle Creek, as well as in the park itself at Boltons Green.

To the north and inland from the timber town of Geeveston is the Tahune AirWalk. Here visitors can stroll amongst the treetops, looking out over the Huon River. There are a number of forest drives in the area, with some routes providing access to secluded campsites.

On the west coast camping is possible at Macquarie Heads near Strahan while experienced walkers can camp along the walking track to Frenchmans Cap.

The preferred time for camping and walking in this region is late spring, summer and early autumn, especially the inland lakes and coastal walks.

BEST Campsites!

Edgar Campground
Southwest National Park

Land of the Giants Campground
Mt Field National Park

Cockle Creek Campground
Recherche Bay Nature Recreation Area

Boltons Green Campground
Southwest National Park

Esperance camping site
Southern Forests

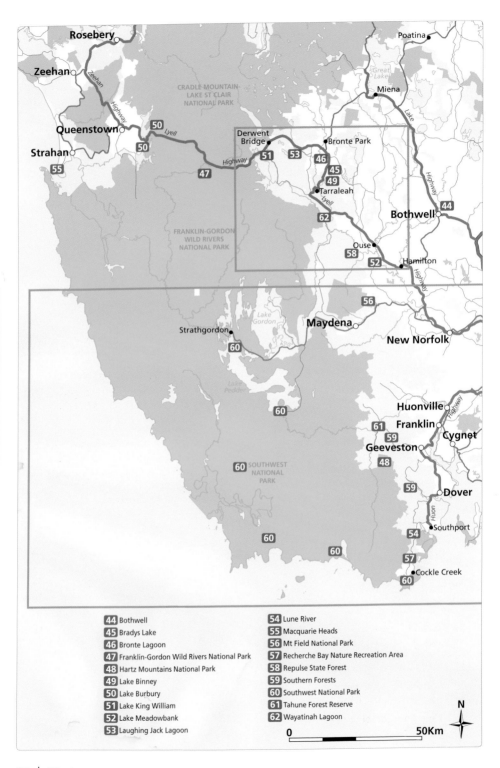

Rosebery
Zeehan
Queenstown
Strahan
Poatina
Miena
CRADLE MOUNTAIN-
LAKE ST CLAIR
NATIONAL PARK
Derwent Bridge
Bronte Park
50
50
47
51 53
46
45
49
Tarraleah
62
Bothwell
44
FRANKLIN-GORDON
WILD RIVERS
NATIONAL PARK
Ouse
58
52
Hamilton
55
56
Lake Gordon
Maydena
New Norfolk
Strathgordon
60
Lake Pedder
60
Huonville
61
59
Franklin
Cygnet
Geeveston
48
SOUTHWEST
NATIONAL
PARK
60
59
Dover
Southport
54
60
60
57
Cockle Creek
60

44	Bothwell	54	Lune River
45	Bradys Lake	55	Macquarie Heads
46	Bronte Lagoon	56	Mt Field National Park
47	Franklin-Gordon Wild Rivers National Park	57	Recherche Bay Nature Recreation Area
48	Hartz Mountains National Park	58	Repulse State Forest
49	Lake Binney	59	Southern Forests
50	Lake Burbury	60	Southwest National Park
51	Lake King William	61	Tahune Forest Reserve
52	Lake Meadowbank	62	Wayatinah Lagoon
53	Laughing Jack Lagoon		

N

0   50Km

44 Bothwell

Founded by the Scots in 1824, the village of Bothwell has over 50 buildings, built mainly by convict labour, that are classified or recognised by the National Trust. As well the village is home to Australia's oldest golf course. Bothwell is situated on the A5 Highway, 76km north of Hobart.

Bothwell Camping Ground

Located in Market Place, Bothwell. Gas/fuel stove only. Key access to showers. Laundry facilities.

GPS S:42 22.967 E:147 00.483
MR: Map 7 C6

FURTHER Information

Central Highlands Council
Tel: 03 6259 5503
Web: www.centralhighlands.tas.gov.au
Bothwell Garage
Tel: 03 6259 5599
Camping fees: Unpowered from $10.00 per site/night. Powered from $15.00 per site/night. Fees payable and keys available at council office, Alexander Street, Bothwell during hours of Mon to Fri 9am to 4.30pm, or from Bothwell Garage outside of these hours.

45 Bradys Lake

Bradys Lake is popular with fisherfolk and watersports enthusiasts. Access to the lake is signposted along the A10 highway south of the A10 and B11 highways junction.

Bradys Lake camping area

Signposted access off the A10 highway, 6.3km south of the A10 and B11 highways junction. There are two access tracks, one south of the canal and one north of the canal, which lead into dispersed bush camping beside the lake. Suitable for big rigs. Use of portable toilets recommended. Bring drinking water and firewood. Gas/stove preferred.

GPS S:42 14.043 E:146 29.708
MR: Map 7 A5

FURTHER Information

Hydro Tasmania
Tel: 1300 360 441
Web: www.hydro.com.au
Maximum stay: 7 days.

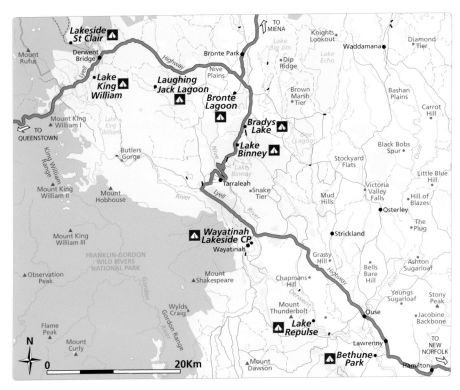

46 Bronte Lagoon

Bronte Lagoon is located to the west of the A10 highway. Access is signposted off the A10 highway 200m south-east of its junction with the B11 highway. The lagoon is a popular fishing and boating destination.

Bronte Lagoon camping area

Signposted access off the A10 highway, 200m south of its junction with the B11 highway. Then travel in 2km to boat ramp and campsites, or cross the dam wall and travel for a further 400m to more sites. Camp only in designated areas. No facilities, suitable for self-sufficient campers only. Use of portable toilets recommended. Bring drinking water and firewood. Gas/stove preferred.

GPS S:42 11.197 E:146 28.768
MR: Map 7 A5

FURTHER Information

> **Hydro Tasmania**
> **Tel:** 1300 360 441
> **Web:** www.hydro.com.au
> **Maximum stay:** 7 days.

Protecting the Franklin, Gordon, Jane and Denison rivers, Franklin-Gordon Wild Rivers National Park is part of the Tasmanian Wilderness World Heritage Area. The majority of the park is rugged and remote, however there are numerous stop-offs along the Lyell Highway which provide access to the park's natural sites including magnificent rainforests, the scenic Nelson Falls, the wild Franklin and Collingwood Rivers. There are spectacular views from Donaghys Hill Wilderness Lookout. For more experienced walkers there is the multi-day Frenchmans Cap Track which leads to the summit of the 1443-metre Frenchmans Cap.

Nelson Falls

Frenchmans Cap Track camping areas

Frenchmans Cap walkers must register and deregister at trackhead. Carry large scale maps. Contact ranger for further details. Walkers must be prepared for dramatic weather changes. Experienced self-sufficient walkers with high level of fitness only. Trackhead and walker registration signposted along the Lyell Highway, 3km west of the Franklin River Bridge, 30km west of Derwent Bridge and 40km east of Queenstown. Gas/fuel stove only.

Trackhead **GPS** S:42 12.507 E:145 58.856
MR: Map 6 J5
Loddon River and Philps Creek: No facilities prior to Lake Vera.
Lake Vera: 16km from trackhead. Hut with coal heater, coal supplied.
Lake Tahune: 9km from Lake Vera. Hut with metho heater, limited metho supplied. Carry own.
Frenchmans Cap: 1km from Lake Tahune. No camping.

FURTHER Information

Parks & Wildlife Service Queenstown
Tel: 03 6471 2511
Parks Pass: Required.

Hartz Mountains National Park

Hartz Mountains National Park offers magnificent views across to the southern coast and over remote mountain ranges. The park has a variety of landscapes including waterfalls and highland lakes, formed during past ice ages by glaciers. The diverse landscapes provide habitat for rainforest, alpine heath and eucalypt forests. Walk to one of the glacial lakes or to the higher ranges for panoramic views. Hartz Peak is the highest peak in the park at 1255m. Access to Hartz Mountains National Park is signposted along the C632 road 13km west of Geeveston, then travel 13.5km south to the car park and picnic area. Visitors need to be aware of and prepared for extreme weather changes.

Hartz Mountains bush camping

Walk-in bush camping is allowed within the park as per Parks and Wildlife bush camping regulations (must be 500m from any road or day use area). Self-sufficient walkers only. Bring drinking water. Gas/ fuel stove only.

Car park **GPS** S:43 13.039 E:146 46.234
Car park **MR:** Map 11 B4

FURTHER Information

Parks & Wildlife Service Huonville
Tel: 03 6264 8460
Parks Pass: Required.
All walkers must register and de-register at information booth within the park. Walkers need to carry large scale maps, contact ranger for further details.

49 Lake Binney

This large lake is situated beside the A10 highway and provides fishing and boating opportunities. Access to Lake Binney's main boat ramp is signposted off the A10 highway, 3km south of Bradys Lake.

Lake Binney camping area

Signposted access off the A10 highway, 3km south of Bradys Lake. A small bush camping area is located beside the highway near the boat ramp. Further bush campsites are located on the lake's eastern shore and can be accessed off the road that crosses the dam wall. Use of portable toilets recommended. Bring drinking water and firewood. Gas/fuel stove preferred.

GPS S:42 15.321 E:146 28.679
MR: Map 7 A5

FURTHER Information

Hydro Tasmania
Tel: 1300 360 441
Web: www.hydro.com.au
Maximum stay: 7 days.

THE SOUTH-WEST WILDERNESS

Duckhole Lake Walk, Southern Forests

Lake Burbury is a large water storage area of 54 square kilometers to the north and south of the A10 highway and situated east of Queenstown. The waters from Lake Burbury travel for seven kilometers through a tunnel to the John Butters Power Station on the banks of the King River. Access to the lake is signposted along the A10 highway east of Queenstown and provides boating and fishing opportunities.

Lake Burbury camping area

Signposted access along the A10 highway, 20.7km east of Queenstown and 86km west of Derwent Bridge. Then drive in 700m to large camping area with limited shade. Suitable for big rigs. Gas/fuel stove only.

GPS S:42 05.808 E:145 40.490
MR: Map 6 H4

FURTHER Information

> **Lake Burbury Camping Area Caretaker**
> **Tel:** 03 6471 2762. Telephone contact available after 5.30pm.
> **Camping fees:** From $5.00 per site/night. Fees payable to Caretaker.

THE SOUTH-WEST WILDERNESS

Thureau Hills camping area

GPS S:42 08.634 E:145 39.026
MR: Map 6 H5

FURTHER Information

> **West Coast Council, Queenstown**
> **Tel:** 03 6471 5880

Signposted access to boat ramp and camping area along the A10 highway, 15km east of Queenstown. Then drive 3.6km south to the camping area, which has limited tent-based camping and is best suited for camper trailers, caravans, motorhomes and campervans. Suitable for big rigs. Bring drinking water and firewood.

Thureau Hills camping area

COLLECTING Firewood

 Most camping areas, especially the more popular ones, are usually devoid of any firewood. If firewood is not supplied by the land managers, it's best to collect enough wood for your needs well before getting to your campsite, or to bring some from home. Please do not cut down any trees, either living or dead, from around the camping area.

THE SOUTH-WEST WILDERNESS

Lake King William is a water storage area situated to the west of Derwent Bridge, and is part of the Derwent Catchment to supply water to the Tarraleah Power Station. The lake is a popular angling site for trout and is accessed off the A10 highway.

Lake King William bush camping

Access tracks to Lake King William are off the A10 highway, 1.7km and 3.7km south of Derwent Bridge Hotel. The northern access track, 1.7km south of Derwent Bridge, leads in 100m to bush campsites around the top of the lake. The southern access track, 3.7km south of Derwent Bridge, leads in 900m to a boat ramp with bush camping in the vicinity. Note: limited motorhome and campervan access to this southern area due to narrow access track with some overhanging vegetation. Bring drinking water. Gas/fuel stove preferred.

Northern sites **GPS** S:42 08.842 E:146 13.074
Southern sites **GPS** S:42 09.522 E:146 12.964
MR: Map 6 K5

FURTHER Information

Hydro Tasmania
Tel: 1300 360 441
Web: www.hydro.com.au
Maximum stay: 7 days.

THE SOUTH-WEST WILDERNESS

Lake Meadowbank is another of the water storage areas within the Derwent Catchment which includes 16 dams and 10 power stations, along with a number of canals, tunnels, weirs and pipelines. Access to the lake is along the Dunrobin Bridge Road, which is signposted along the A10 highway, 7km south of Ouse and 7km north-west of Hamilton. The lake is popular for fishing, canoeing, swimming, water-skiing and boating.

Bethune Park camping area

Access signposted through gate, 2km west of the A10 highway along the Dunrobin Bridge Road (Ellendale Road/ C608 road), at the western end of the bridge. Grassed area on the western foreshore of the lake, suitable for big rigs in the top parking area. Boat ramp on lake's eastern shore. Bring drinking water and firewood. Gas/fuel stove preferred.

GPS S:42 32.180 E:146 43.824
MR: Map 7 B7

FURTHER Information

Hydro Tasmania
Tel: 1300 360 441
Web: www.hydro.com.au
Maximum stay: 7 days.

This interestingly named lagoon is a storage area within the Derwent Catchment. Access to Laughing Jack Lagoon is signposted on the A10 highway, 20km east of Derwent Bridge via the C602 road, and is a favoured fishing destination.

Laughing Jack Lagoon bush camping

Signposted access along the A10 highway, 20km east of Derwent Bridge and 6.2km west of the B11 highway. From the A10 highway travel south along the C602 road for 2.6km, then turn into the signposted C602 and follow it for 6.8km to dam wall. At dam wall a track on left leads to bush campsites best suited for tents and off-road camper trailers. Track on right at dam wall crosses bridge and leads to further sites. Use of portable toilets recommended. Bring drinking water and firewood. Gas/fuel stove preferred.

GPS S:42 10.614 E:146 19.920
MR: Map 6 K5

FURTHER Information

Hydro Tasmania
Tel: 1300 360 441
Web: www.hydro.com.au
Maximum stay: 7 days.

THE SOUTH-WEST WILDERNESS

Big Tree Reserve, Styx River

At Lune River is the **Ida Bay Railway**, the last of the many bush tramways built in Tasmania. The historic 1940s locos and passenger carriages travel along a 7km section of narrow gauge railway to the end of the line at Deep Hole and Elliott's Beach, where there are marked walking tracks and a scenic beach. En route you will view historic sites beside the railway including the original town site of Ida Bay along with scenic forests. Ida Bay Railway is located at Lune River on the C636 road, 7km south of the A6 highway.

Ida Bay Railway camping area

Signposted access along the C636 road 7km south of the A6 highway. Communal cabin with full cooking facilities, heating and lounge area. Laundry facilities and cafe.

GPS S:43 26.605 E:146 54.219
MR: Map 11 C6

FURTHER Information

Ida Bay Railway
Tel: 03 6298 3110. Bookings preferred.
Web: www.idabayrailway.com.au
Camping fees: From $10.00 per person/night.

55 Macquarie Heads

Macquarie Heads is the northern head of the mouth of the Macquarie Harbour. The heads are located 15km south of the historic port town of Strahan. Fishing at the heads is a very popular past time.

Macquarie Harbour, Strahan

Macquarie Heads camping area

Located at the end of the C251 (Macquarie Heads Road), 14km south of Strahan. Access is signposted from Strahan. Unsealed access road, which can be rough at times. Suitable for big rigs. Bring own fire drum/pot and firewood.

GPS S:42 13.213 E:145 14.268
MR: Map 5 F5

FURTHER Information

Macquarie Heads Caretaker =
Tel: 03 6471 7382. Telephone contact available between 5pm and 8pm.
Camping fees: From $10.00 per site/night.

THE SOUTH-WEST WILDERNESS

Located just over an hours drive from Hobart, Mt Field National Park is one of Tasmania's oldest national parks. The park protects a diverse range of flora of tall swamp gum forests, rainforests and tree ferns, which in turn provides a habitat to a variety of wildlife including quolls, bandicoots, possums and bettongs. Visitors to Mt Field National Park can enjoy a number of walking trails through magnificent fern forests and to the scenic Russell Falls, or walk or drive to the historic Government Huts in the Lake Dobson area of the park. The park's camping area is situated beside the Tyena River and visited by kangaroos and pademelons during the morning and afternoon. Access to the park is signposted along the C609 road which is signposted off the B61 road at Westerway, 29km north-west of New Norfolk.

Land of the Giants Campground

Signposted access along the Lake Dobson Road (C609), 7.6km west of Westerway, which is situated on the B61 road, 29km north-west of New Norfolk. Then drive in 1km to the large, grassed and shaded camping area, and the national park visitor centre. Suitable for big rigs.

Laundry facilities. Gas/fuel stove only.
GPS S:42 41.072 E:146 42.955
MR: Map 7 B8

FURTHER Information

Parks & Wildlife Service Mt Field
Tel: 03 6288 1149
Parks Pass: Required.
Camping fees: Unpowered from $16.00 per site/night for 2 people. Powered from $20.00 per site/ night for 2 people. Fees payable at self-registration station.

THE SOUTH-WEST WILDERNESS

Land of the Giants Campground, Mt Field National Park

57 Recherche Bay Nature Recreation Area

This attractive recreation area is situated close to the southern tip of the island. Recherche Bay Nature Recreation Area looks out over the Recherche Bay and has beautiful coastal scenery, excellent swimming, fishing and beach walks. Access is along the Cockle Creek Road (C636), which is signposted off the A6 highway 3km north of Southport. The first camping area is 21km along the C636 road from the A6.

Gilhams Beach campground

Signposted access along Cockle Creek Road, 14.2km south of the Ida Bay Railway. Suitable for big rigs. Bring drinking water and firewood.

GPS S:43 32.526 E:146 53.532

MR: Map 11 C6

Recherche Bay Nature Recreation Area

Finns Beach campground

Signposted access along Cockle Creek Road, 800m south of Gilhams Beach access track. Suitable for big rigs. Bring drinking water and firewood.

GPS S:43 32.895 E:146 53.263
MR: Map 11 C6

Catamaran River campground

Signposted access along Cockle Creek Road, 1.1km south of Finns Beach access track. Suitable for big rigs. Bring drinking water and firewood.

GPS S:43 33.276 E:146 53.269
MR: Map 11 C6

Cockle Creek campground

Signposted access along Cockle Creek Road, 3km south of Catamaran River campground and north of bridge at Cockle Creek. Suitable for big rigs. Bring drinking water and firewood. **NB:** South side of bridge is Southwest National Park - pets not permitted the national park.

GPS S:43 34.659 E:146 53.214
MR: Map 11 C6

FURTHER Information

> **Parks & Wildlife Service Huonville**
> **Tel:** 03 6264 8460
> **Parks Pass:** Not required.
> **Maximum stay:** 1 month.

58 Repulse State Forest

Forest area on western foreshore of Lake Repulse. To reach the forest, take the Ellendale Road from the A10 highway which is 6.7km south of Ouse. Then take Dawson Road, which is 2.7km west of the highway. Follow Dawson Road for 11.4km to enter the forest. At this reading there is a track on the right which leads to various tracks to the lake's foreshore and bush campsites.

Lake Repulse bush camping

Numerous tracks lead to bush campsites on lake foreshore within the forest. Steep access tracks. Sites suitable for camper trailers with 4WD tow vehicles. Be aware of logging trucks. Some sites have natural boat launches. Bring drinking water and firewood.

Access track **GPS** S:42 30.340 E:146 37.045
MR: Map 7 A7

FURTHER Information

> **Forestry Tasmania Derwent**
> **Tel:** 03 6233 7449

59 Southern Forests

Owing to the high rainfall and rich soils, the Southern Forests comprise mainly of wet eucalypt forests and cloak the valleys of the Weld, Picton, Arve, Huon, Lune and Esperance rivers. Activities include walking, rafting, car touring, fishing and camping.

Esperance camping site

Located 7.7km along Esperance River Road. Esperance River Road is signposted off the A6 highway at Strathblane, which is 4.4km south of the Dover Hotel. Camping on the north side of the Esperance River. Tent-based camping, carry gear from car park into large grassed area with facilities. Vehicle, camper trailer and caravan-based camping at nearby grassed clearings. Water from river, boil first. Some firewood supplied.

GPS S:43 17.950 E:146 54.716
MR: Map 11 C5

Arve River picnic & camping area

Signposted access along Arve Road, 15km west of Geeveston at the Arve River Streamside Reserve. Tent-based camping, carry gear over bollards. Limited space for small camper trailers, caravans and campervans. Water from tank. Some firewood supplied.

GPS S:43 09.515 E:146 48.400
MR: Map 11 B4

FURTHER Information

> **Forestry Tasmania Geeveston**
> **Tel:** 03 6297 0012

Esperance camping site, Southern Forests

Point Hibbs
Lowren
Hill
Innes
Peak
Olegas
Bluff
The
Twins
Moores
Landing
Warounrim
Plains
Thirkell
Hill
Mount
Lewis
Hamilton Range
Lake
Gordon
Adamsfield
Hazell
Hill
Mount
Robert
Atkins
Range
Ibsens
Peak
FRANKLIN-GORDON
WILD RIVERS
NATIONAL PARK
Mount
Sprent
Strathgordon
High Rocky Point
SOUTHWEST
CONSERVATION
AREA
Jones
Mistake
Ted's
Beach
Mount
Cullen
Mount
Osmund
Mount
Eleanor
Koruna
Peak
Mount
Helder
Mount
Wedge
Brown
Hill
View
Hill
Lake
Pedder
Mount
Cawthorn
Sentinel
Range
Mount
Jean
Top
Plain
Double
Peak
Hardwood
Hill
Mount
Solitary
Rookery
Plain
Frankland
Peak
Scotts
Peak
Low Rocky Point
Elliott
Bay
Elliott
Hill
SOUTHWEST
NATIONAL
PARK
Long
Ridge
Edgar
Cinder
Hill
Huon
Propstring Range
Piners
Peak
Mount
Gaffney
Corner
Peak
Sculptured
Mountain
Elliott Point
Mount
Hayes
Mount
Scorpio
Brier Holme Head
Castle
Hill
Davey
Sugarloaf
Mount
Robinson
Mount
Sirius
Mount
Hean
Davey
Gorge
Mount
Braddon
Svenor Point
Mount
Legge
Toogee
Hill
Mount
King
Mount
Wilson
Ripple
Mountain
North Head
Pt St Vincent
Mount
Stokes
Mount
Rugby
High Round
Mountain
SOUTHERN
OCEAN
Hilliard Head
Mount
Nicholls
Mount
Beattie
Mount
Fulton
Ray
Range
Lone
Hill
Mount
Rallinga
Melaleuca
Flying Cloud Point
Mount
Melaleuca
Mount
Counsel
South West
Cape
Telopea
Point
Cox
Bluff
Red
Point
Maatsu
Grou

60 Southwest National Park

Covering over six hundred thousand hectares of remote wild country, Southwest National Park is Tasmania's largest national park. In the south of the park is Cockle Creek which is the start/finish of the South Coast Track. Other shorter walks can also be enjoyed from here. In the north of the park are the excellent trout fishing lakes of Lake Gordon and Lake Pedder. Visit the Gordon Dam and Hydro visitor centre.

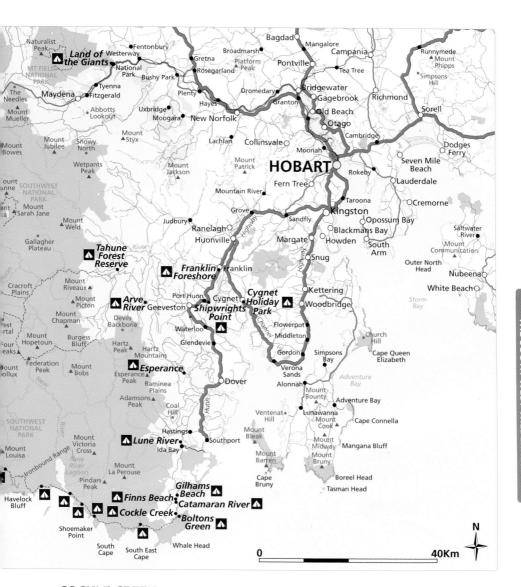

COCKLE CREEK

Boltons Green Campground

Located on Cockle Creek Road on south side of bridge at Cockle Creek, 20km south of Lune River. Suitable for big rigs.

Ranger on site during summer. Bring drinking water. Gas/fuel stove only.

GPS S:43 34.963 E:146 53.701
MR: Map 11 C7

FURTHER Information

Parks & Wildlife Service Huonville
Tel: 03 6264 8460
Parks Pass: Required.

Boltons Green Campground

LAKE PEDDER

Edgar Campground

Signposted access 30.3km along
Scotts Peak Dam Road (C607), which
is signposted off the B61 road. Scotts
Peak Dam Road is signposted off the
B61 road 43km east of Strathgordon
and 50km west of Westerway. Grassed
camping area with 10 sites and some
shade. Carry insect repellant. Boat ramp
located nearby at Scotts Peak Dam. Some
firewood supplied.
GPS S:43 01.803 E:146 21.004
MR: Map 10 F3

FURTHER Information

Hydro Tasmania
Tel: 1300 360 441
Web: www.hydro.com.au
Maximum stay: 7 days.

Huon Campground

Signposted access 6km west of Edgar Campground along the Scotts Peak Dam Road. Then drive in 1km to the small, well-protected camping area with 7 sites. Boat ramp nearby at Scotts Peak Dam. Trackhead for the Port Davey Walking Track. Bring drinking water. Some firewood supplied.

GPS S:43 02.265 E:146 18.087
MR: Map 10 E3

Teds Beach Campground

Signposted access on Strathgordon Road (B61 road), 38km west of Scotts Peak Dam Road and 3km east of Strathgordon. Limited tent-based camping. Gas/fuel stove only.

GPS S:42 47.219 E:146 03.660
MR: Map 10 D1

FURTHER Information

> **Parks & Wildlife Service Mt Field**
> **Tel:** 03 6288 1149
> **Parks Pass:** Required.
> **Camping fees:** Huon CG from $10.00 per site/night. Teds Beach CG from $13.00 per site/night.

Teds Beach Campground

SOUTHWEST NATIONAL PARK WALKING TRACKS

Port Davey Track camping areas

Walking track from Scotts Peak to Melaleuca, 3-4 days. Trackhead and walkers registration at Huon Campground on Scotts Peak Dam Road (C607) off the B61 Road. Self-sufficient experienced walkers. Gas/fuel stove only.

Trackhead **GPS** S:43 02.265 E:146 18.087
Trackhead **MR:** Map 10 E3
Huon Campground: See page 107.
Junction Creek
Crossing River
Spring River
Bathurst Narrows
Melaleuca: Toilet and walker's huts located here.

South Coast Track camping areas

Walking track from Cockle Creek to Melaleuca, 6-8 days. Trackhead and walkers registration at Cockle Creek on Cockle Creek Road. Self-sufficient experienced walkers. Gas/fuel stove only.

Trackhead **MR:** 11 C7
Cockle Creek: See Boltons Green, page 105.
South Cape Rivulet
Granite Beach (east)
Surprise Bay
New River Lagoon Boat Crossing
Deadman's Bay
Louisa River
Point Eric
Melaleuca: Toilet and walker's huts located here.

FURTHER Information

> **Parks & Wildlife Service Huonville**
> **Tel:** 03 6264 8460
> **Parks Pass:** Required.
> All walkers must register and de-register at registration booths. Walkers need to carry large scale maps, contact ranger for further details and for details of other walking tracks.

61 Tahune Forest Reserve

This beautiful reserve is on the banks of the Huon River and home to the popular Tahune Forest AirWalk. The AirWalk winds through the forest 20 metres above ground level. Huon pines can been seen along the Huon Pine Walk. The Tahune Forest AirWalk and Visitor Centre is located 30km north-west of Geeveston along the Arve Road.

Tahune Forest Reserve camping area

Located adjacent to the Tahune AirWalk car park at the end of Arve Road, 30km north-west of Geeveston. Small camping area with 5 sites suitable only for campervans and motorhomes. All facilities are located at the nearby visitor centre.

GPS S:43 05.684 E:146 43.847
MR: Map 11 B3

FURTHER Information

> **Tahune Forest AirWalk and Visitor Centre**
> **Tel:** 03 6297 0068. Campers need to check in at the Visitor Centre's front counter on arrival.
> **Camping fees:** From $20.00 per vehicle/night.
> **Maximum stay:** 2 nights.

Tahune Forest AirWalk, Tahune Forest Reserve

62 Wayatinah Lagoon

Located north of New Norfolk with signposted access off the Lyell Highway (A10). Wayatinah is home to the six station Lower Derwent hydro-electric scheme. The lagoon offers good trout fishing.

Wayatinah Lakeside Caravan Park

Signposted access along Wayatinah Road in Wayatinah. Wayatinah Road is signposted off the A10 highway, 38km north of Hamilton. Camp kitchen, pool, tennis court and laundry facilities. Bring firewood.

GPS S:42 23.148 E:146 30.330
MR: Map 6 L6

FURTHER Information

Wayatinah Lakeside Caravan Park
Tel: 03 6289 3317. Bookings essential during school holidays and long weekends.
Camping fees: Unpowered from $20.00 per site/night for 2 people. Powered from $25.00 per site/2 people

The Rugged North-West

SITED IN THE PATH OF 'THE ROARING Forties' as they blow in from the Southern Ocean, the rugged North-West of Tasmania offers spectacular coastal scenery, sweeping plains and vast tracts of old-growth forest of the Tarkine. These weather conditions often create ideal surfing conditions, making this region a popular destination for keen board riders and windsurfers. The region also offers some of the best car touring in the state.

BEST Campsites!

Manuka Campground
Arthur-Pieman Conservation Area

Prickly Wattles Campground
Arthur-Pieman Conservation Area

Black River camping area
Peggs Beach Conservation Area

O'Neils Creek Reserve
Gowrie Park

Montagu Camping Ground
Montagu Recreation Reserve

The remote and wild Arthur-Pieman Conservation Area runs along the west coast, taking in the Arthur and Pieman rivers, and offers some great camping and fishing. There are a number of campsites here to choose from. In the south is the one-time gold mining settlement of Corinna. Situated on the scenic Pieman River, there are boat cruises available along the river, or if you have your own water transport a boat ramp is located near the ferry. Majestic Huon pines can be seen along the river's edge growing in their natural environs. It's even said that the forests along the river are home to the last of the thylacine!

On the north coast facing Bass Strait are Montague Recreation Reserve and Peggs Beach Conservation Area. Here swimming, fishing and beachcombing can be enjoyed over the warmer months.

Located in the centre of the region is the township of Waratah, once home to one of the world's richest tin mines, while in the east is the delightful town of Sheffield, with its beautiful colourful murals. Both towns offer camping for travellers.

You can enjoy this region year round, however the warmer months of the year tend to be the most popular and are probably the best time to visit as winter can be cold and windy at times.

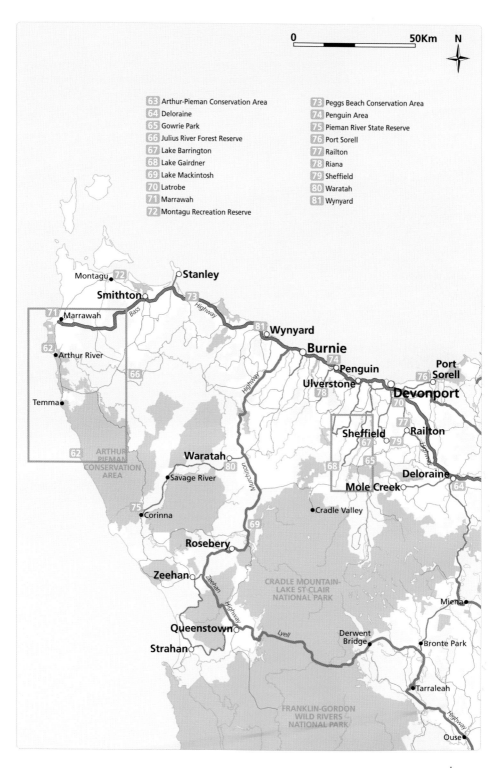

63 Arthur-Pieman Conservation Area
64 Deloraine
65 Gowrie Park
66 Julius River Forest Reserve
67 Lake Barrington
68 Lake Gairdner
69 Lake Mackintosh
70 Latrobe
71 Marrawah
72 Montagu Recreation Reserve

73 Peggs Beach Conservation Area
74 Penguin Area
75 Pieman River State Reserve
76 Port Sorell
77 Railton
78 Riana
79 Sheffield
80 Waratah
81 Wynyard

THE RUGGED NORTH-WEST

Located on the north-west coast. Access is from Smithon via the A2 to Marrawah then travel south along the C214. This large conservation area of 100 000 hectares covers the region between the Arthur River in the north and the Pieman River in the south. Activities include fishing, diving, sea kayaking and surfing.

Manuka Campground

Signposted access along Arthur River Road, 200m north of Arthur River ranger base. Suitable for big rigs. Boil water first. Bring firewood.

GPS S:41 02.721 E:144 40.109
MR: Map 1 C5

Manuka Campground

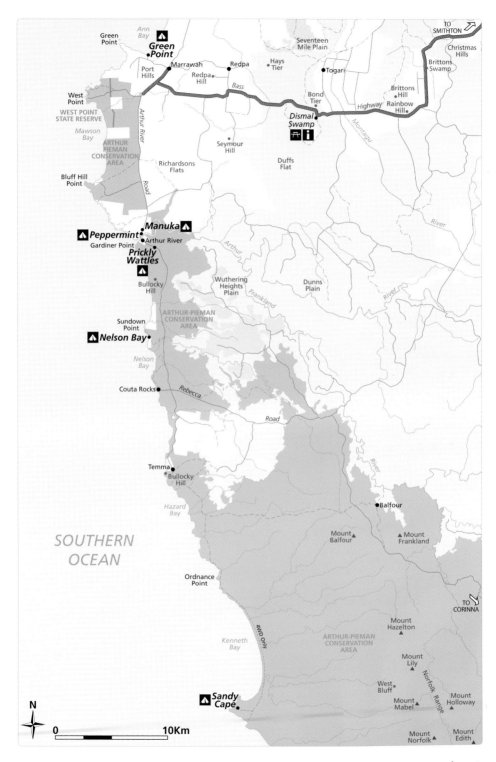

TO
SMITHTON

Green
Point

Ann
Bay

Green
Point

Christmas
Hills

Marrawah

Redpa

Seventeen
Mile Plain

Brittons
Swamp

Port
Hills

Redpa
Hill

Hays
Tier

Togari

Brittons
Hill

West
Point

Bass

Bond
Tier

Highway

Rainbow
Hill

WEST POINT
STATE RESERVE

Mawson
Bay

Arthur River

Dismal
Swamp

Montagu

River

ARTHUR
PIEMAN
CONSERVATION
AREA

Seymour
Hill

Duffs
Flat

Bluff Hill
Point

Richardsons
Flats

Road

Manuka

Arthur

River

Peppermint

Gardiner Point

Arthur River

Prickly
Wattles

Wuthering
Heights
Plain

Frankland

Dunns
Plain

River

Bullocky
Hill

Sundown
Point

ARTHUR-PIEMAN
CONSERVATION
AREA

Nelson Bay

Nelson
Bay

Couta Rocks

Rebecca

Road

River

Temma

Bullocky
Hill

Balfour

Hazard
Bay

Mount
Balfour

Mount
Frankland

SOUTHERN
OCEAN

Ordnance
Point

TO
CORINNA

Mount
Hazelton

Kenneth
Bay

ARTHUR-PIEMAN
CONSERVATION
AREA

Mount
Lily

West
Bluff

Mount
Holloway

N

Sandy
Cape

Mount
Mabel

Norfolk Range

0   10Km

Mount
Norfolk

Mount
Edith

Peppermint Campground

Signposted access along Arthur River Road in Arthur River village, next to ranger base. Limited trailer and caravan sites, best suited for tent-based camping. Bring drinking water and firewood.

GPS S:41 02.877 E:144 40.055
MR: Map 1 C5

Prickly Wattles Campground

Signposted access along Arthur River Road, 2km south of the Arthur River ranger base. Boil water first. Bring firewood.

GPS S:41 03.550 E:144 40.825
MR: Map 1 C5

Prickly Wattles Campground

Nelson Bay Campground

Signposted access along the C214 road, 10.7km south of Arthur River ranger base. Travel east for 2.3km to road junction. Camping to the right on grassed area. Suitable for self-sufficient campers, as site is near private huts and cabins. Bring drinking water and firewood. Carry own firepot or brazier. Use of portable toilets recommended.

GPS S:41 07.748 E:144 40.330
MR: Map 1 C6

Sandy Cape camping area

Located 50km south of Arthur River and 26km south of Temma. 4WD access only via Temma or via the Balfour Track off the Corinna Road. Well-equipped/experienced 4WD only. Contact Ranger for track conditions and to obtain an Off Road Authority for travel to Sandy Cape. Swimming beach nearby. Bring drinking water and firewood.

GPS S:41 25.667 E:144 45.700
MR: Map 1 C7

THE RUGGED NORTH-WEST

Bush camping areas

Walk-in bush camping throughout the park is allowed. Carry large scale maps and contact Parks office for further details. Bring drinking water. Gas/fuel stove preferred.

FURTHER Information

Parks & Wildlife Service
Arthur River
Tel: 03 6457 1225
Parks Pass: Not required.
Camping fees: Manuka, Peppermint and Prickly Wattles CGs from $13.00 per site/night up to 2 adults. Other unserviced sites from $6.00 per site/night up to 2 adults. Fees payable at Arthur River ranger base during work hours. Use self-registration box at ranger base after hours.

64 Deloraine

Deloraine is situated at the foothills of the Great Western Tiers on the Meander River, 54km west of Launceston and 50km south-east of Devonport. Classified by the National Trust, there are many beautifully restored Georgian and Victorian buildings in and around the town.

Deloraine Overnight Park

Signposted access along Racecourse Road, which is signposted off East Parade in Deloraine. Sullage dump point here. Designated area for fully self-contained motorhomes ie: units must have own fresh water storage, sealed grey water holding tank, sealed black water.
MR: Map 3 B8

FURTHER Information

Meander Valley Council
Tel: 03 6393 5300
Maximum stay: 24 hours.

WATER Wise

Fresh water for drinking and cooking is one aspect of camping which needs to be taken into consideration. You can't always rely on creeks and rivers – they may be polluted by animals, muddy or even dry. Allow around 7 litres of water per person per day – plus a couple of extra litres if you are heading into remote areas. We find storing water in a couple of 20 litre containers more convenient than in one larger container. Besides being easier to lift in and out of the vehicle and easier to handle around camp, if one container springs a leak you don't risk losing all your drinking water

The small village of Gowrie Park is located 14km south of Sheffield and accessed via the C136.

O'Neills Creek Reserve

FURTHER Information

Sheffield Visitor Information Centre
Tel: 03 6491 1036
Camping fees: From $5.00 per site/night.
Maximum stay: 4 nights.

Signposted access along the C136 road in Gowrie Park, 14km south of Sheffield. Suitable for big rigs. Bring drinking water and firewood.
GPS S:41 28.007 E:146 13.191
MR: Map 2 K8

O'Neills Creek Reserve

THE RUGGED NORTH-WEST

Julius River Forest Reserve

Julius River Forest Reserve is located 46km south of Smithton. Access to the reserve is along the South Arthur Forest Drive which is signposted from the A2 highway at Smithton. Enjoy a walk through the cool temperate rainforest.

Julius River Forest camping area

Located 10km east of Kanunnah Bridge over Arthur River and 600m east of the Julius River Forest picnic area. Gravel road commences 1.8km east of Kanunnah Bridge. Six sites best suited for camper trailer, caravan, motorhome and campervan camping. Not suitable for tent based camping. Toilet facilities in picnic area.

GPS S:41 09.131 E:145 02.048
MR: Map 1 E6

FURTHER Information

> **Forestry Tasmania, Smithton**
> **Tel:** 03 6452 4900

THE RUGGED NORTH-WEST

This large lake is a popular venue for water-skiing, rowing, canoeing, fishing, boating and swimming. Located to the south of Devonport, access to the eastern shore is via West Kentish and to the western shore via Lower Wilmot. Camp only in the designated areas.

Kentish Park camping area

Located on the eastern shore of Lake Barrington, 6km west of West Kentish. Access is signposted off the C140 road south of Sheffield. Bring firewood.

GPS S:41 22.900 E:146 31.100
MR: Map 2 K7

Lake Barrington Park camping area

Located on the western shore of Lake Barrington, east of Wilmot and 8km south of Lower Wilmot. From Lower Wilmot travel south for 4.4km and take signposted Buxtons Road. Follow this road for 2.7km and turn into Lake Barrington Road, and after 600m track on right leads up hill to grassed camping area. Bring firewood.

GPS S:41 22.678 E:146 12.647
MR: Map 2 K7

FURTHER Information

Sheffield Visitor Information Centre
Tel: 03 6491 1036
Maximum stay: 21 days in a 2 month period.

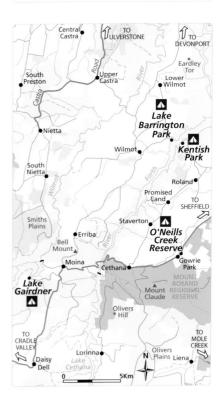

THE RUGGED NORTH-WEST

Located to the west of Moina. Access is off the C132 road, 1km south of Moina.

Lake Gairdner camping area

The access road (which is not signposted) is off the C132 road, 1km south of Moina. From the C132 travel for 4km to a small grassed area in the vicinity of bridge over Iris River. Open area with no shade. Bring drinking water and firewood.

GPS S:41 29.033 E:146 03.561

MR: Map 2 J8

FURTHER Information

> **Hydro Tasmania**
> **Tel:** 1300 360 441
> **Web:** www.hydro.com.au
> **Maximum stay:** 7 days.

Lake Mackintosh is adjacent to the town of Tullah. The lake is a hydro dam which offers anglers top-rate trout fishing.

Lake Mackintosh camping area

Located north of the dam wall via Mackintosh Dam Road, 6.3km north of Tullah. Dam road is signposted in Tullah. Site not accessible when dam water is flowing over spillway. Best suited for camper trailers, caravans, motorhomes and campervans, limited tent-based camping. No facilities, suitable for self-sufficient campers. Bring drinking water and firewood.

GPS S:41 41.129 E:145 39.396

MR: Map 6 H2

FURTHER Information

> **Hydro Tasmania**
> **Tel:** 1300 360 441
> **Web:** www.hydro.com.au
> **West Coast Council**
> **Tel:** 03 6471 4700
> **Maximum stay:** 7 days.

THE RUGGED NORTH-WEST

Lake Mackintosh camping area, Lake Mackintosh

70 Latrobe

Situated on the banks of the Mersey River, Latrobe's main street has 75 heritage-listed buildings. Other attractions of this historic town include the Australian Axemans Hall of Fame, scenic parklands, antiquities and crafts, fine foods and some excellent platypus viewing areas. Latrobe is located west of the Bass Highway with access signposted off the highway 20km south-east of Devonport.

Latrobe Motorhome Stop

Signposted access on Cotton Street in Latrobe. Designated area for fully self-contained motorhomes ie: units must have own fresh water storage, sealed grey water holding tank, sealed black water.
MR: Map 2 L6

FURTHER Information

Latrobe Visitor Information Centre
River Road, Bells Parade, Latrobe
Tel: 03 6421 4699. Permit required from visitor information centre.
Web: www.latrobetasmania.com.au
Maximum stay: 48 hours.

Suspension Bridge, Montezuma Falls, south of Rosebery

Marrawah is located 51km west of Smithton via the Bass Highway (A2). The coastline's rugged headlands receive the full force of the Roaring Forties from the Southern Ocean. Popular swimming, board riding and windsurfing area.

Green Point camping area

Located 2.4km west of Marrawah. Access via Beach Road off Green Point Road. Outdoor cold showers. Bring drinking water and firewood.
GPS S:40 54.566 E:144 40.738
MR: Map 1 C4

FURTHER Information

Circular Head Council
Tel: 03 6452 4800
Web: www.circularhead.tas.gov.au

Green Point camping area

THE RUGGED NORTH-WEST

Montagu is located 15km west of Smithton along the C215 road. This coastal location is popular for water activities. Rips can be common, check with caretakers for safe swimming, fishing, canoeing and water-skiing sites.

Montagu Camping Ground

Located 4km north of Montagu. Accessed along Old Port Road, which is signposted off the C215 road 1km east of Montagu locality. Bring drinking water and firewood.

GPS S:40 44.735 E:144 58.643
MR: Map 1 D3

FURTHER Information

Caretaker
Tel: 0428 524 843. Bookings recommended for Christmas, long weekends and Easter. Camping area open from 1 November to 30 April. Opening dates may vary from year to year.

Circular Head Council
Tel: 03 6452 4800
Web: www.circularhead.tas.gov.au
Camping fees: From $10.50 per site/night up to 2 people.

Montagu Camping Ground

THE RUGGED NORTH-WEST

Located on the north coast between Stanley and Wynyard. Activities include fishing, swimming and beachcombing.

Black River camping area

Signposted access along the A2 (Bass Highway), 8.8km east of the Stanley turn-off (B21) and 2.2km west of Peggs Beach turn-off. Drive in 700m to start of camping areas. Suitable for big rigs. Very large area with some open and some shaded sites. Natural boat launch into river. **NB:** No fires on the ground, carry own firepot or brazier. Limited tank water, bring own drinking water and firewood.

GPS S:40 50.721 E:145 19.199
MR: Map 1 F4

Peggs Beach camping area

Signposted access along the A2 (Bass Highway), 2.2km east of Black River turn-off and 42km west of Wynyard. Camping area close to road. Limited sites for travellers as the camping area has permanent holiday sites. Beach boat launch nearby. Tank water, boil first or bring own drinking water. Bring firewood.

GPS S:40 51.199 E:145 21.030
MR: Map 1 F4

FURTHER Information

Parks & Wildlife Service Smithton
Tel: 03 6452 4998
Parks Pass: Not required.
Camping fees: From $13.00 per site/night up to 2 people.

Black River camping area

THE RUGGED NORTH-WEST

74 Penguin Area

Penguin is home to the large under cover Penguin Market which is held every Sunday showcasing a wonderful array of arts and crafts along with fresh produce. Situated between Devonport and Burnie, access to Penguin is signposted along the Bass Highway.

Halls Park

Signposted access along the Bass Highway at Sulphur Creek, 8km west of Penguin. Designated area for fully self-contained caravans, motorhomes and campervans ie: units must have own fresh water storage, sealed grey water holding tank, sealed black water.
MR: Map 2 J5

Penguin Lions Park

Small area located at Pengiun Lions Park, access is along Preservation Drive opposite the old surf club. Designated area for fully self-contained caravans, motorhomes and campervans ie: units must have own fresh water storage, sealed grey water holding tank, sealed black water.
MR: Map 2 J5

FURTHER Information

Penguin Visitor Information Centre
Tel: 03 6437 1421
Maximum stay: 48 hours.

75 Pieman River State Reserve

Corinna has a rich history, magnificent wilderness, bushwalks and good trout fishing. Take time out to enjoy a river cruise along the Pieman. Access to Corinna from the north is via the C247 road from Savage River (26km) or the C249 road (80km) which is 58km south of Smithton. From the south access is via the C249 road from Zeehan (48km), ferry crossing is required. Caravans note: maximum length (combination wheel base) for ferry is 9 metres.

Corinna Campground

Located in Corinna. Access via Savage River or Smithton from the north and via Zeehan from the south. Limited water, bring drinking water. Firewood supplied. No power.
GPS S:41 39.031 E:145 04.717
MR: Map 5 E1

FURTHER Information

Corinna Wilderness Experience
Tel: 03 6446 1170. Limited campsites. Bookings essential from November to May.
Web: www.corinna.com.au
Camping fees: From $20.00 per site/night for 2 people. Cabin accommodation available.

Corinna Campground, Pieman River State Reserve

76 Port Sorell

Located 15km east of Devonport on the Rubicon River estuary. Close to Bass Strait beaches and popular water activities area.

Port Sorell Lions Club Caravan Park

Located on Meredith Street in Port Sorell on the eastern banks of Rubicon River. Fire pots and firewood available. Laundry facilities and childrens playground.

MR: Map 3 A6

FURTHER Information

Port Sorell Lions Club Caravan Park
Tel: 03 6428 7267 Bookings essential for peak periods, November to April.
Web: www.portsorellcaravanpark.com.au
Camping fees: Unpowered from $15.00 per site/night for 2 people. Powered from $30.00 per site/night for 2 people.

The town of Railton is located 13km south of Latrobe and 12km north-east of Sheffield. Walk the streets of Railton and enjoy the imaginative topiary display of over 100 figures in this unique outdoor gallery.

Railway Park

Access is along the Esplande in Railton. Designated area for fully self-contained caravans and motorhomes ie: units must have own fresh water storage, sealed grey water holding tank, sealed black water.
MR: Map 2 L7

FURTHER *Information*

Kentish Visitor Information Centre, Sheffield
Tel: 03 6491 1036
Web: www.kentish.tas.gov.au
Maximum stay: 4 nights.

Riana is a small village in a dairy and produce region south of Penguin. Access via the B17 road from Penguin. Visit the nearby deer farm.

Riana Pioneer Park camping ground

Signposted access on Pine Road (B17) in Riana, 17km south of Penguin. Drinking water, bore water. Some firewood supplied.
GPS S:41 12.933 E:145 50.933
MR: Map 2 J6

FURTHER *Information*

Riana Pioneer Park Secretary/ Caretaker
Tel: 03 6111 4779 or 03 6437 6137
Camping fees: Unpowered from $8.00 per site/night for 2 people. Powered from $14.00 per site/night for 2 people. Fees collected daily.

THE RUGGED NORTH-WEST

The Nut, Stanley

Sheffield is known as 'The Town of Murals' and is situated 33km south of Devonport. There is a self-guided audio tour of the town's 50 beautiful murals depicting the life of a small Tasmanian rural town. As the gateway to Cradle Mountain, Sheffield is a wonderful base from which to explore and enjoy the region.

Sheffield Recreation Ground

Access is along Spring Street in Sheffield. Designated area for fully self-contained caravans and motorhomes ie: units must have own fresh water storage, sealed grey water holding tank, sealed black water.

MR: Map 2 K7

FURTHER Information

Kentish Visitor Information Centre, Sheffield
Tel: 03 6491 1036
Web: www.kentish.tas.gov.au
Maximum stay: 4 nights.

Sheffield

Located 67km south of Burnie via the Hampshire-Guildford Road. Waratah was once home to the world's richest tin mine and is only five minutes drive west of the Murchison Highway. The area has many activities for the visitor including gold panning, trout fishing and river cruises.

Waratah camping ground

Located on Smith Street in Waratah, behind council offices. Key access to toilet and shower facilities.

GPS S:41 26.733 E:145 31.967
MR: Map 1 G8

FURTHER Information

Waratah-Wynyard Shire Council, Waratah
Tel: 03 6439 7100. Hours: Mon to Fri 9am-5pm
Web: www.warwyn.tas.gov.au
Waratah Roadhouse
Tel: 03 6439 1110
Camping fees: Unpowered site from $21.00 per site/night. Powered site from $27.00 per site/night. A refundable key bond is required. Key available from council offices during business hours or from roadhouse after hours.

A former mining town, Wynyard is now a major service centre for the state's north-west. Located 12km west of Burnie, Wynyard is situated on the coast at the mouth of the Inglis River. Visit Fossil Bluff, Table Cape Lookout, enjoy a scenic walk along the Inglis River or try your luck fishing for trout in the Inglis and Flowerdale rivers.

Wynyard Showgrounds

Access on Jackson Street in Wynyard. Designated area for fully self-contained motorhomes ie: units must have own fresh water storage, sealed grey water holding tank, sealed black water.
MR: Map 2 H5

FURTHER Information

Waratah-Wynyard Shire Council, Wynyard
Tel: 03 6443 8333. Hours: Mon to Fri 9am-5pm
Web: www.warwyn.tas.gov.au
Wynyard Visitor Information Centre
Tel: 03 6443 8330
Maximum stay: 24 hours.

THE RUGGED NORTH-WEST

The Central Highland Lakes

THE CENTRAL HIGHLAND LAKES
region offers some of the state's most
magnificent mountain country. Visitors to
the region have the opportunity to enjoy
a stroll along one of a number of walking
trails ranging from easy day walks – many
are in the vicinity of Dove Lake at Cradle
Mountain and Lake St Clair – to longer
multi-day hikes such as the internationally
famous Overland Track. In the centre of
the region are the alpine wilderness areas
of Walls of Jerusalem National Park and
to the west is the world-renowned Cradle
Mountain – Lake St Clair National Park,
both offering excellent walking routes
through breathtaking alpine scenery.

Further to the east, the numerous man-made
lakes of the Central Plateau offer excellent
fishing and boating opportunities. Those lucky
enough may enjoy a catch of trout from one of
the renown trout fisheries such as Great Lake,
while those looking for seclusion can seek out
remote camping sites on the banks of Woods
Lake or Lagoon of Islands.

In the north of the region are Marakoopa
and King Solomons Caves, both located within
Mole Creek Karst National Park, while the
interestingly named Devils Gullet is on the
Great Western Tier.

Visitors should remember that weather
conditions in the central highlands can change
drastically, and must be prepared for all
weather conditions, including snow, at any
time of the year. It is not uncommon to have
four seasons in a number of hours in some
locations throughout this region. Late spring,
summer and autumn are the preferred times to
visit this diverse area.

BEST Campsites!

**Lake St Clair – Lake St Clair Tourist
Park**
Cradle Mountain – Lake St Clair
National Park

Lower Liffey Reserve campsite
Liffey Falls State Reserve

Lagoon of Islands bush camping
Lagoon of Islands

Lake Parangana bush camping
Lake Parangana

Pumphouse Bay Camping Ground
Arthurs Lake

Located within the Central Plateau Protected Area, Arthurs Lake is a haven for the keen fisherfolk. Access to Arthurs Lake is along the Poatina Road (B51), south of Poatina and north of the A5 highway.

Pumphouse Bay Camping Ground

Signposted access along the Poatina Road (B51), 6km north of the A5 junction and 36km south of Poatina. Then drive in 800m to camping area. Woodfired hot showers, generally October to April. Boil drinking water first. Gather own firewood.

GPS S:41 59.116 E:146 51.640
MR: Map 7 C3

Pumphouse Bay Camping Ground

Jonah Bay Camping Ground

Signposted access along the Poatina Road (B51), 4.2km north of the Pumphouse Bay access road and 32km south of Poatina. Then drive in 3.1km to road junction, turn right and follow for 1.7km to camping area. Grassed, shaded sites beside the lake. Bring drinking water and firewood.

GPS S:41 57.522 E:146 54.150
MR: Map 7 C3

Jonah Bay Camping Ground

FURTHER Information

Bothwell Tourism Association
Tel: 03 6287 1313
Camping fees: Pumphouse Bay: from $4.00 per adult/night. Jonah Bay: from $3.00 per adult/night. Fees payable at self-registration stations.

THE CENTRAL HIGHLAND LAKES

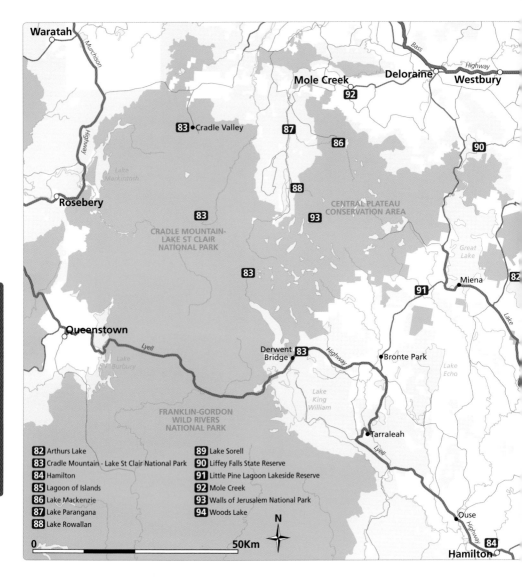

82 Arthurs Lake
83 Cradle Mountain - Lake St Clair National Park
84 Hamilton
85 Lagoon of Islands
86 Lake Mackenzie
87 Lake Parangana
88 Lake Rowallan
89 Lake Sorell
90 Liffey Falls State Reserve
91 Little Pine Lagoon Lakeside Reserve
92 Mole Creek
93 Walls of Jerusalem National Park
94 Woods Lake

0   50Km

N

CRADLE MOUNTAIN Day Walks

There are four popular day walks that can be undertaken by visitors to Cradle Mountain. Of these, easily the most popular is the 2 hour (6km) Dove Lake Circuit—this easy grade walk will take you right around Dove Lake with superb vistas of Cradle Mountain. Those after a short stroll (20 minutes) may wish to amble along the Enchanted Walk which starts at the visitor centre and meanders through old growth rainforest.

The Crater Lake Circuit Walk is a 2 hour walk and a good option for cold, wet and windy days as it is more protected. Serious day walkers can tackle the Cradle Mountain Summit Walk, an 8 hour return climb to the imposing peak of Cradle Mountain via Lake Lilla and Marions Lookout.

Details of these walks plus a host of others around the state can be found in the *Tasmania's 60 Great Short Walks* brochure.

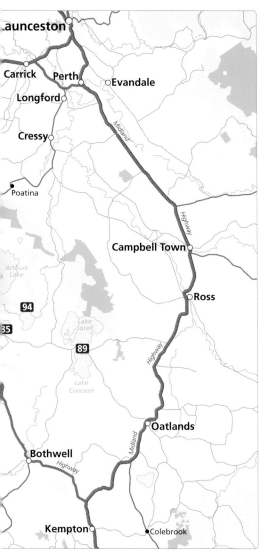

RECREATIONAL
Fishing Licences

If you intend dangling a line in the hope of
hooking a tasty trout in Tasmania's inland
waterways then you are required to obtain a
Recreational Fishing Licence. These are available
in selected centres or by contacting the Inland
Fisheries Service on 03 6233 4140 or at
www.ifs.tas.gov.au for details.

Cradle Mountain

83 Cradle Mountain – Lake St Clair National Park

Cradle Mountain – Lake St Clair National Park is one of Tasmania's most popular parks with many visitors coming to walk the world-renowned Overland Track. The park features the rugged contours of Cradle Mountain and its surrounding alpine environs as its northern centerpiece while to the south is Lake St Clair, the deepest lake in Australia, with its beautiful forests. This large national park is part of the Tasmanian Wilderness World Heritage Area. Numerous day walks of varying lengths are also on offer.

Cradle Mountain – Discovery Holiday Park Cradle Mountain

Signposted access along Cradle Mountain Road, 54km south-west of Sheffield and 2km before park's entry station. Suitable for big rigs. Camp kitchen and laundry facilities.

GPS S:41 34.788 E:145 56.198
MR: Map 6 I1

FURTHER Information

Discovery Holiday Park Cradle Mountain
Tel: 03 6492 1395. Bookings for powered sites recommended during peak period, November to May.
Web: www.discoveryholidayparks.com.au
Parks Pass: Not required.
Camping fees: Contact office for current fee structure. This park offers off-peak, peak and shoulder periods. Cabin and backpacker accommodation available.

Lake St Clair – Lake St Clair Tourist Park

Signposted access along Lake St Clair Road, 5km north-west of the Lyell Highway (A10) at Derwent Bridge. Token-operated showers, tokens from office. Laundry facilities. Firewood supplied.

GPS S:42 06.925 E:146 10.630
MR: Map 6 K4

FURTHER Information

Lake St Clair Lodge and Tourist Park
Tel: 03 6289 1137. Bookings for powered sites recommended during January.
Web: www.lakestclairlodge.com.au
Parks Pass: Required.
Camping fees: Contact office for current fee structure. This park offers off-peak, peak and shoulder periods. Cabin and backpacker accommodation available.

THE CENTRAL HIGHLAND LAKES

Lake St Clair — Lake St Clair Tourist Park

The Overland Track camping areas

Six-day walking track from Cradle Valley to Lake St Clair. Self-sufficient experienced walkers. Gas/fuel stove only. Rainwater tanks at huts. Remember: Pack it in/Pack it out.

Cradle Valley **MR:** Map 6 I1
Waterfall Valley Hut: 10km from Waldheim (6 hours)
GPS S:41 421.884 E:145 56.812
Windermere Hut: 7.5km from Waterfall Valley Hut (3 hours)
GPS S:41 46.295 E:145 57.376
New Pelion Hut: 16.5km from Windermere Hut (6 hours)
GPS S:41 49.772 E:146 02.781
Kia Ora Hut: 10km from New Pelion Hut (3 hours)
GPS S:41 53.531 E:146 04.890
Bert Nichols (Windy Ridge) Hut: 10km from Kia Ora Hut (4 hours)
GPS S:41 56.024 E:146 05.256
Narcissus Hut: 9km from Bert Nichols Hut (3 hours)
GPS S:42 00.752 E:146 06.097
Lake St Clair **MR:** Map 6 K4
Side trip camping areas:
Scott Kilvert Memorial Hut at Lake Rodway
Pine Valley Hut at Pine Valley
Echo Point Hut at Echo Point

FURTHER Information

Parks & Wildlife Service Visitor Centres

Cradle Mountain **tel:** 03 6492 1110
Lake St Clair **tel:** 03 6289 1172
A booking system and fee applies to walk the Overland Track from 1 November to 30 April. Outside of this period bookings and fees do not apply. Bookings can be made over the phone contact Parks & Wildlife Service on **tel:** 03 6233 6047, or online by visiting website: www.overlandtrack.com.au, or in person at the above visitor information centres.
Parks Pass: Required.
Overland Track Fees: From $200.00 per adult and $160.00 per child (5 to 17 years)/ seniors/pension consessionaires.
NB: All walkers must register and deregister at trackheads, it is also recommended to have a nominated contact person. Carry large scale maps. There are a number of specialised walking publications for the Overland Track.

Cradle Mountain day walk

84 Hamilton

The historic village of Hamilton is located on the A10 highway 75km north-west of Hobart beside the Clyde River. There are numerous historic buildings dating as far back as the 1830s, many of which were built of local sandstone by convict labor.

Hamilton Caravan Park

Signposted access along River Street (Tarleton Street) in Hamilton at the western end of town. Coin-operated showers. Grassed areas. Laundry facilities, key access.

GPS S:42 33.550 E:146 49.833
MR: Map 7 C7

FURTHER Information

Central Highlands Council
Tel: 03 6286 3202. Key access to laundry, refundable key deposit applies. Key available from council offices located on Tarleton Street.
Web: www.centralhighlands.tas.gov.au
Maximum stay: From $5.00 per site/night.

85 Lagoon of Islands

Situated in the Central Plateau region, access to the Lagoon of Islands is via the Interlaken Road off the A5 Highway. Popular fishing spot.

Lagoon of Islands bush camping

Signposted access along the C527 (Interlaken Road), 4.1km east of the A5 and 48km west of the A1 highway. Then drive in 300m to dam wall and dispersed bush campsites around lake's edge. Sheltered, shady grassed areas. Bring drinking water. Gas/fuel stove preferred.

GPS S:42 06.707 E:146 56.083
MR: Map 7 C4

FURTHER Information

Hydro Tasmania
Tel: 1300 360 441
Web: www.hydro.com.au
Maximum stay: 7 days.

THE CENTRAL HIGHLAND LAKES

Lagoon of Islands camping area, Lagoon of Islands

86 Lake Mackenzie

Access via Lake Mackenzie Road off the C171 road, which leaves the C138 road, 20km west of Mole Creek. Travel for 22km to this open campsite and fishing area.

Lake Mackenzie bush camping

Located 22km along Lake Mackenzie Road at the dam. Lake Mackenzie Road is signposted off the C171 road 300m south of its junction with the C138. Access road may be closed during bad weather. Limited tent-based camping due to rocky ground. Suitable for off-road camper trailers. Small exposed site best suited to anglers. Gas/fuel stove preferred. Bring drinking water and firewood.

GPS S:41 40.594 E:146 22.763
MR: Map 6 L1

FURTHER Information

Hydro Tasmania
Tel: 1300 360 441
Web: www.hydro.com.au
Maximum stay: 7 days.

87 Lake Parangana

Lake Parangana is located to the west of Mole Creek and accessed off the C171, which is signposted 20km west of Mole Creek. The lake's access track is through the picnic area which is 7.4km south of the C171 and C138 junction, and 1.2km south of the dam wall.

Lake Parangana bush camping

Access road is 1.2km south of the Parangana Dam wall through the picnic area, 7.4km along the C171 road. Dispersed bush camping on western foreshore of lake. Some open sites and some good protected sites back from the water among vegetation. Gas/fuel stove preferred. Bring drinking water, or boil from lake. Bring firewood.

GPS S:41 38.642 E:146 13.515
MR: Map 6 K1

FURTHER Information

Hydro Tasmania
Tel: 1300 360 441
Web: www.hydro.com.au
Maximum stay: 7 days.

Lake Rowallan is situated south of Lake Parangana and is accessed off the C171, which is signposted 20km west of Mole Creek. The lake's dam wall is 9.7km south of the Lake Parangana access track. Bush camping on the lake's eastern foreshore south of the dam and bush campsites beside the river north of the dam.

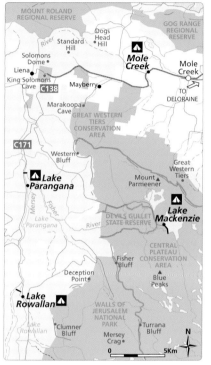

Lake Rowallan bush camping

Located south of Lake Parangana and accessed along the C171. Numerous access tracks lead off the C171 to bush camping areas on the lake's eastern foreshore south of the dam wall, and beside the river north of the dam wall. Boat ramps are signposted on the south side of the dam wall. Bring drinking water, or boil water from lake or river. Bring firewood. Gas/fuel stove preferred.

GPS S:41 44.142 E:146 13.176
MR: Map 6 K2

FURTHER Information

Hydro Tasmania
Tel: 1300 360 441
Web: www.hydro.com.au
Maximum stay: 7 days.

THE CENTRAL HIGHLAND LAKES

Lake Sorell is within the Central Plateau Conservation/Protected area. Access from the east is via the gravel Interlaken road (C526) off the A1 highway (this road has some steep sections and is not recommended for caravans), 12km south of Ross or the Interlaken road (C527) from Oatlands. Access is also possible via the C527 road from Bothwelll to the south and from the west via the C528 off the A5 highway.

Dago Point camping area

Signposted access along the Interlaken Road at Interlaken, 26.4km west of the A1 via the C526 and 26km east of the A5 via the C527. Turn-off is 2.5km west of the C528 (Bothwell) road. Then drive in 300m to playground and toilet block, turn left for 200m to reach large camping area with shaded and grassed individual sites. Bring firewood.

GPS S:42 07.887 E:147 09.914
MR: Map 7 D4

FURTHER Information

Parks & Wildlife Service Liawenee
Tel: 03 6259 8148
Parks Pass: Not required.
Camping fees: From $4.00 per adult/night

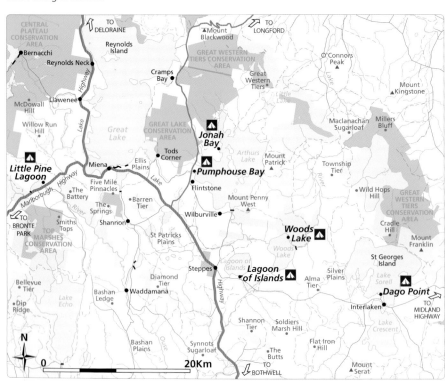

This scenic reserve is nestled on the slopes of the Great Western Tiers amongst rainforest. Along with Liffey Falls there are a number of smaller falls within the reserve. Enjoy the nature walk through tree ferns and tall eucalypts. The reserve is 15km west of Bracknell and 7km west of the locality of Liffey. Accessed along the C513, from the west off the A5 and from the east via Gulf Road/Liffey Road (C513).

Lower Liffey Reserve campsite

Camping area located at the lower carpark of Liffey Falls. Access is signposted off the C513 road, 7km west of the locality of Liffey – this is the recommended access for caravans, trailers and motorhomes. Alternative access can be made from the west off the A5 (this access road has steep and narrow sections). Access from the A5 highway is signposted 23km south of Deloraine. From the highway travel for 1.9km to a Y-junction. The road on the right at junction leads to the falls top carpark and walking track (this road is not suitable for trailers, caravans or motorhomes). At junction keep left and follow the signposting to Liffey for a further 5.8km to the signposted Liffey Falls/Lower Track road. Then drive in 700m to the nicely shaded and grassed camping area. Bring drinking water and firewood.

GPS S:41 40.994 E:146 46.932
MR: Map 7 B1

FURTHER Information

Parks & Wildlife Service Prospect
Tel: 03 6336 5312
Parks Pass: Not required.

Lower Liffey Reserve campsite

THE CENTRAL HIGHLAND LAKES

91 Little Pine Lagoon Lakeside Reserve

Located south-west of Miena, Little Pine Lagoon Lakeside Reserve is accessed along the B11 road, 7.4km south of its junction with the A5 highway. The B11 road is signposted off the A5 2.6km west of Miena and 67km south of Deloraine. The reserve is located close to the road and offers fishing and boating opportunities.

Little Pine Lagoon Lakeside Reserve camping area

Signposted access along the B11 road, 7.4km south of the A5 highway. Then drive in 500m from B11 to self-registration station and camping areas. One area for camper trailers and caravans, and one area for tent-based camping. Bring drinking water. Gas/fuel stove only.

GPS S:41 59.977 E:146 36.696
MR: Map 7 A4

FURTHER Information

Parks & Wildlife Service Liawenee
Tel: 03 6259 8148
Parks Pass: Not required.
Camping fees: From $3.00 per adult/night. Fees payable at self-registration station.

Little Pine Lagoon camping area

THE CENTRAL HIGHLAND LAKES

Mole Creek is an ideal location to base yourself whilst exploring the nearby lakes and King Solomons and Marakoopa caves. Mole Creek is on the B12 road 23km west of Deloraine.

Mole Creek Caravan Park

Signposted access at junction of B12 and C137 roads, 3.2km west of Mole Creek village. Situated beside creek. Coin-operated showers. Camp kitchen and laundry facilities. Fires only allowed on the creek side of the camping area. Firewood supplied.

GPS S:41 33.101 E:146 21.629
MR: Map 6 L1

FURTHER Information

Mole Creek Caravan Park
Tel: 03 6363 1150
Web: www.molecreek.net.au
Camping fees: Unpowered from $20.00 per site/night for 2 people. Powered from $25.00 per site/night for 2 people. Fees payable to caretaker. On-side accommodation available.

Mole Creek Caravan Park

THE CENTRAL HIGHLAND LAKES

Woods Lake

93 Walls of Jerusalem National Park

The park features majestic mountain scenery and alpine lakes. There is no vehicle access within the park—day or overnight walkers only. The park is 23km from the C171 junction via the Walls of Jerusalem Track off the Mersey Forest Road (C171). The C171 is 20km west of Mole Creek. Walkers must be aware and ready for dramatic weather changes whilst visiting this park.

Wild Dog Creek walk-in camping area

Located 2 to 3 hours walk from car park. Access to car park is signposted along the C171 road. Walk-in bush campsites for self-sufficient walkers. Some tank water. Gas/fuel stove only.
MR: Map 6 K2

FURTHER Information

Parks & Wildlife Service Mole Creek
Tel: 03 6363 5133
Parks Pass: Required.
Walkers must register and deregister at registration station along track near car park and carry large scale maps. Contact ranger for further details and information.

94 Woods Lake

Woods Lake is a popular fishing and boating destination, with remote bush camping around the lake's foreshore. Access to Woods Lake is signposted off Arthurs Lake Road (C525), which is signposted off the B51 highway 4.5km north of the B51 and A5 highway junction, and 38km south of Poatina. The lake's foreshore is located 12km south-east of its turn off from Arthurs Lake Road. Unsealed access road can be rough. AWD or 4WD vehicle recommended, especially if towing.

Woods Lake bush camping

From the B51 highway take the signposted Arthurs Lake Road (C525) for 8.6km to the signposted Woods Lake access track. Then travel for 1.2km to a Y-junction and keep right along the signposted Woods Lake road. Travel for 11km to Woods Lake boat ramp and to numerous tracks which lead to bush campsites along the lake's foreshore. No facilities, suitable for self-sufficient campers. Bring drinking water and firewood.
GPS S:42 03.878 E:147 00.902
MR: Map 7 C4

FURTHER Information

Hydro Tasmania
Tel: 1300 360 441
Web: www.hydro.com.au
Maximum stay: 7 days.

Roadside Rest Areas

REST AREA/TOWN	LOCATION	TOILET	TABLE	FIREPLACE	SHELTER	WATER	MAP
NORTH-EAST REGION							
Blue Tier Picnic Area	Lottah Road, 4k N of Lottah	✓	✓	✓	✓		4 I6
Conaro Rest Area	Midland Highway 10km N of Campbell Town	✓	✓	✓	✓	✓	7 F2
Derby Park Picnic Area	On A3 at western end of town	✓	✓	✓	✓		4 G6
Evercreech Forest Reserve Picnic Area	13.4km NE of Mathinna on Egans Road via Clayton Road	✓	✓	✓	✓		4 H7
Halls Falls Picnic Area	On Anchor Road, 900m N of the A3		✓				4 I6
Hardings Falls Forest Reserve Picnic Area	Turn off is 36.1km N of the B34 road via the MS and MG roads, and 25.5km N of Meetus Falls	✓	✓				8 I3
Hollybank Forest Picnic Area	20km NE of Launceston via the B81	✓		✓	✓		3 D7
Lookout/Picnic Area	On A3 highway 14km N of Targa and 16km S of Scottsdale	✓	✓	✓	✓		3 E6
Maa Mon Chin Picnic Area	3.5km W of Weldborough Hotel via Mount Paris Dam Road						4 H6
Mathinna Falls Picnic Area	10.1km N of Mathinna on Waterfall Gully Road, via Clayton Road	✓	✓				4 H7
Minnie Jessop Picnic Ground	2.2km west of Maa Mon Chin Picnic Area via Mount Paris Dam Road				✓		4 H6
Parramatta Creek Rest Area	Bass Highway S of Sassafras	✓	✓	✓	✓	✓	2 L6
Ralphs Falls Picnic Area	18.6km W of Pyengana via Ringarooma Road	✓	✓	✓	✓	✓	4 H6
Springfield Picnic Area	13.3km south of Scottsdale via the C406 South Springfield Road		✓	✓			3 F6
SOUTH-EAST REGION							
Cradoc Park Picnic Area	Cradoc on the B68 highway, south of Huonville	✓	✓		✓		11 D3
Denison Canal Park	On A9 highway at Dunalley	✓	✓		✓		12 G2
Gordon Jetty Picnic Area	On B68 road at Gordon	✓	✓	✓			11 E4
Mavista Picnic Area, Bruny Island	On Resolution Road, which is 2.1km S of Adventure Bay via Lockleys Road	✓	✓				11 E5
Meetus Falls Picnic Area	On MS Road, which is 10.6km N of the B34 road		✓	✓	✓		8 H3
Sandspit Picnic Area	On Wielangta Road Forest Drive, 15km N of the A9		✓	✓	✓		12 H1
Spring Beach Picnic Area	Access off the C320 road, 4.2km S of Orford	✓	✓	✓	✓		8 H7
St Peters Pass Rest Area	Midland Highway, 3km S of Woodbury and 10km N of Oatlands	✓	✓	✓	✓	✓	7 E5
Three Thumbs Picnic Area	Access off Wielangta Forest Drive, 5km S of the A3 at Orford		✓		✓	✓	8 H8

REST AREAS

REST AREA/TOWN	LOCATION	TOILET	TABLE	FIREPLACE	SHELTER	WATER	MAP
SOUTH-WEST REGION							
Calvert Park Picnic Area	Beside Huon River at Judbury, 13km W of Huonville via Glen Huon Road	✓	✓	✓	✓		11 C3
Ellendale Picnic Area	Located at fire station in village of Ellendale on C608 road	✓	✓	✓	✓		7 B8
Glen Huon Memorial Park	8.9k mW of Huonville via Glen Huon Road		✓		✓		11 C3
Grace Nicholas Park	At northern end of bridge in village of Ouse on A10 highway		✓		✓	✓	7 B7
Henty Dunes Picnic Area	Signposted access of B27 highway, 13km N of Strahan		✓		✓		5 F4
Nive River Picnic Area	On A10 highway at power station, 3.3km N of the northern access road to Tarraleah	✓	✓	✓	✓	✓	6 L6
Swan Basin Picnic Area	9.4km S of Strahan along C251 road		✓	✓			5 F5
A1 – QUEENSTOWN TO DERWENT BRIDGE							
Nelson Falls Walking Track	27km E of Queenstown	✓					6 H4
Donaghy Hill Lookout & Walk	51km E of Queenstown						6 I5
B61 ROAD – MAYDENA TO STRATHGORDON							
Styx Valley Big Tree Reserve	Turn off is 3km W of Maydena, then 15km S						11 A1
Needles Picnic Area	24km W of Maydena	✓	✓		✓		10 L1
Boyd Lookout	3.4km W of Scotts Peak Dam Road						10 K1
Mt Wedge Walking Track	12.6km W of Scotts Peak Dam Road						10 K2
Wedge River Picnic Area	17.8km W of Scotts Peak Dam Road	✓	✓	✓	✓	✓	10 K2

REST AREAS

Blue Tier Picnic Area

REST AREA/TOWN	LOCATION	TOILET	TABLE	FIREPLACE	SHELTER	WATER	MAP
NORTH-WEST REGION							
Alma Reserve Picnic Area	Beside river on Wilmot Road, 12.4km S of Forth		✓	✓			2 K6
Dip Falls Picnic Area	On C225 road, 11.9km S of Mawbanna and 26.6km S of A2 highway	✓	✓	✓	✓		1 F5
Fossey River Rest Area	On A10 highway, 2km S of B23 junction	✓	✓	✓	✓		2 H8
Hellyer Gorge State Reserve Rest Area	On A10 highway, 39km S of A2	✓	✓		✓		2 H6
Leven Canyon Picnic Area	Access along C128 road, 9km SW of Nietta	✓	✓	✓		✓	2 J7
Oldina Picnic Area	Access via C235, 7km SW of Wynyard	✓	✓	✓	✓		2 H5
Peggs Beach Picnic Area	On A2 highway, 1.1km E of Peggs Beach CA	✓	✓	✓			1 F4
Sisters Beach Rest Area	At end of East Boulevard at Sisters Beach	✓	✓	✓	✓		2 G4
Stitt Park Picnic Area	South of Rosebery shopping village beside Stitt River	✓	✓	✓			6 G2
Warrawee Forest Reserve Picnic Area	Beside Mersey River, 6km S of Latrobe	✓	✓	✓			2 L6
SOUTH ARTHUR FOREST DRIVE							
Kanunnah Bridge Picnic Area	Beside Arthur River, 36.5km S of Smithton on B22 road	✓	✓	✓		✓	1 E6
Sumac Lookout	1.8km E of Kanunnah Bridge	✓					1 E6
Julius River Forest Reserve Picnic Area	7.6km E of Sumac Lookout	✓	✓	✓	✓		1 E6
Lake Chisholm Forest Reserve	Walk to lake. Turn off is 2.8km E of Julius River						1 E6
Dempster Lookout	Turn off is 2.8km E of Lake Chisholm turn off						1 E6
Rapid River Picnic Area	Located 4.1km N of Dempster Lookout turn off	✓					1 E6
Milkshakes Forest Reserve Picnic Area	Turn off is 13.7km N of Rapid River PA, then 6.5km to picnic area	✓	✓	✓	✓	✓	1 E5
Tayatea Bridge Picnic Area	Located 5.9km N of Milkshakes Forest Reserve PA access track, SE of Trowutta	✓	✓				1 E5

REST AREAS

REST AREA/TOWN	LOCATION	TOILET	TABLE	FIREPLACE	SHELTER	WATER	MAP
WESTERN EXPLORER – ARTHUR RIVER TO CORINNA							
Gardiner Point Picnic Area	On Airey Street at Edge of the World. Turn off is south of the bridge over Arthur River.	✓	✓				1 C5
Lindsay River Crossing	Small clearing beside the road on south side of bridge, 52.8km S of Arthur River						1 D7
Donaldson River Crossing	Small clearing beside the road on north side of bridge, 82.6km S of Arthur River						1 E8
Longback Walk & Scenic Lookout	Signposted 96.4km S of Arthur River						5 E1
Scenic Lookout	Signposted 99.9km S of Arthur River						5 E1
Guthrie Creek Crossing	Small clearing beside the road on south side of bridge, 104.6km S of Arthur River						5 E1
Corinna Picnic Area	Beside Pieman River near ferry, 110.8km S of Arthur River	✓	✓	✓	✓		5 E1
CENTRAL HIGHLAND LAKES REGION							
Liffey Falls Picnic Area	Picnic area and walking tracks, 5.7km E of A5 highway via C153	✓	✓	✓	✓		7 B2
Meander Forest Reserve Picnic Area	Access via C167, south of Meander	✓	✓	✓	✓		7 A1
Mersey White Water Forest Reserve Picnic Area	Located 7km S of Lake Parangana	✓	✓	✓	✓		6 K1
Steppes Historic Site Picnic Area	Adjacent to historic site at Steppes on A5 highway, 34km N of Bothwell	✓					7 C4

REST AREAS

Milkshakes Forest Reserve Picnic Area

Esperance camping site, Southern Forests

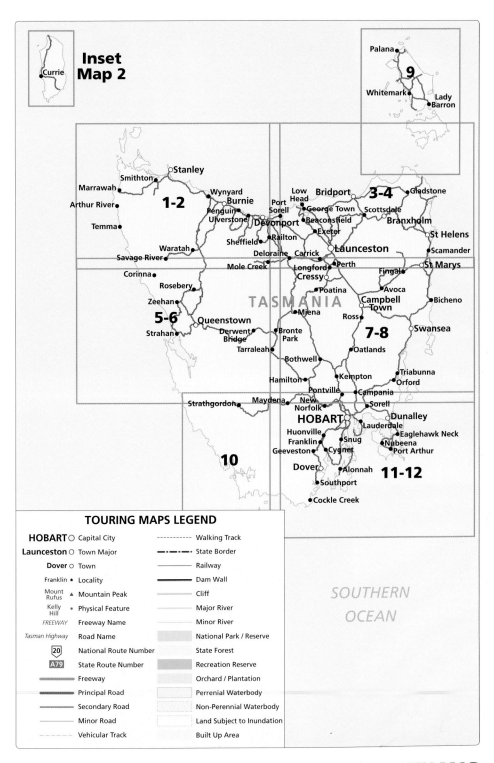

Inset
Map 2

Currie

Palana
9
Whitemark
Lady
Barron

Stanley
Smithton
Marrawah
Wynyard
Low Head
Bridport
3-4
Gladstone
Arthur River
1-2
Burnie
Port Sorell
George Town
Scottsdale
Penguin
Beaconsfield
Branxholm
Temma
Ulverstone
Devonport
Exeter
Railton
St Helens
Sheffield
Launceston
Scamander
Waratah
Deloraine
Carrick
Savage River
Mole Creek
Longford
Perth
St Marys
Corinna
Cressy
Fingal
Rosebery
Poatina
Avoca
Zeehan
Campbell Town
Bicheno
TASMANIA
Mjena
Ross
5-6
Queenstown
Derwent Bridge
Bronte Park
7-8
Swansea
Strahan
Tarraleah
Oatlands
Bothwell
Hamilton
Kempton
Triabunna
Pontville
Orford
Strathgordon
Maydena
New Norfolk
Campania
Sorell
HOBART
Dunalley
Huonville
Lauderdale
Franklin
Snug
Eaglehawk Neck
10
Geeveston
Cygnet
Nubeena
Port Arthur
Dover
Alonnah
11-12
Southport
Cockle Creek

SOUTHERN
OCEAN

TOURING MAPS LEGEND

HOBART ○	Capital City	----------	Walking Track
Launceston ○	Town Major	—·—·—	State Border
Dover ○	Town	————	Railway
Franklin •	Locality	————	Dam Wall
Mount Rufus ▲	Mountain Peak	————	Cliff
Kelly Hill •	Physical Feature	————	Major River
FREEWAY	Freeway Name	————	Minor River
Tasman Highway	Road Name		National Park / Reserve
20	National Route Number		State Forest
A79	State Route Number		Recreation Reserve
═══════	Freeway		Orchard / Plantation
▬▬▬▬▬	Principal Road		Perrenial Waterbody
————	Secondary Road		Non-Perennial Waterbody
————	Minor Road		Land Subject to Inundation
-------	Vehicular Track		Built Up Area

TOURING MAPS

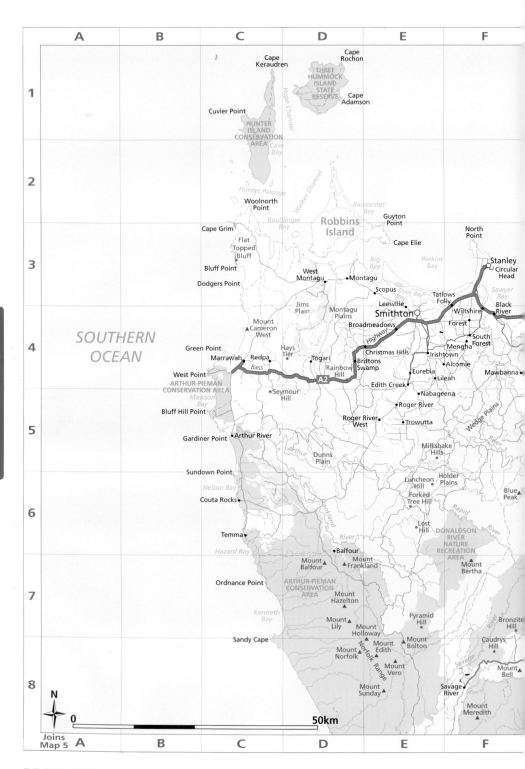

A B C D E F

1

Cape
Keraudren
Cape
Rochon
THREE
HUMMOCK
ISLAND
STATE
RESERVE
Cape
Adamson
Cuvier Point
Hope Channel
HUNTER
ISLAND
CONSERVATION
AREA
Cave
Bay

2

Hunter Passage
Woolnorth
Point
Walker Channel
Ransonnet
Bay
Robbins
Island
Guyton
Point

3

Cape Grim
Flat
Topped
Bluff
Bluff Point
Dodgers Point
Boullanger
Bay
Big
Bay
West
Montagu
Montagu
Scopus
Duck Bay
Perkins
Bay
Cape Elie
North
Point
Stanley
Circular
Head
Sawyer
Bay

4

SOUTHERN
OCEAN
Green Point
Marrawah
Redpa
West Point
ARTHUR-PIEMAN
CONSERVATION AREA
Mawson
Bay
Bluff Hill Point
Mount
Cameron
West
Jims
Plain
Hays
Tier
Bass
Togari
Rainbow
Hill
Montagu
Plains
Broadmeadows
Highway
Smithton
Christmas Hills
Brittons
Swamp
Edith Creek
Leesville
Tatlows
Folly
Forest
Mengha
Irishtown
Eurebia
Lileah
Alcomie
Wiltshire
Black
River
Mawbanna
South
Forest
A2

5

Gardiner Point
Arthur River
Seymour
Hill
Arthur
Dunns
Plain
Roger River
West
Trowutta
Nabageena
Roger River
Milkshake
Hills
Wedge Plains
River

6

Sundown Point
Nelson Bay
Couta Rocks
Temma
Hazard Bay
Frankland River S
Balfour
Mount
Balfour
Mount
Frankland
Luncheon
Hill
Forked
Tree Hill
Lost
Hill
Holder
Plains
Rapid River
DONALDSON
RIVER
NATURE
RECREATION
AREA
Mount
Bertha
Blue
Peak

7

Ordnance Point
ARTHUR-PIEMAN
CONSERVATION
AREA
Mount
Hazelton
Kenneth
Bay
Pyramid
Hill
River
Bronzite

8

Sandy Cape
Mount
Lily
Mount
Holloway
Mount
Norfolk
Mount
Edith
Mount
Vero
Norfolk Range
Mount
Bolton
Mount
Sunday
Savage
Savage
River
Caudrys
Hill
Mount
Bell
Mount
Meredith

N

0   50km

Joins
Map 5   A   B   C   D   E   F

MAP 1 | Camping GUIDE TO **TASMANIA**

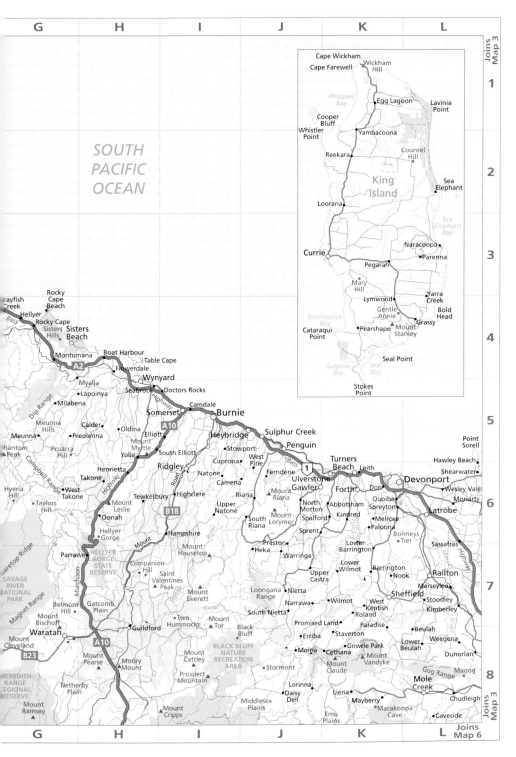

G   H   I   J   K   L

SOUTH
PACIFIC
OCEAN

1

Cape Wickham
Cape Farewell   Wickham
                 Hill

Phoques
Bay   Egg Lagoon   Lavinia
                          Point
Cooper
Bluff
Whistler
Point   Yambacoona

Reekara   Counsel
                         Hill

2   Sea
                            King   Elephant
                            Island

Loorana   Sea
                                     Elephant
                                     Bay

3   Naracoopa
Currie   Parenna

        Pegarah

        Mary   Yarra
        Hill   Creek
Lymwood   Gentle   Bold
                      Annie   Head
Cataraqui   Pearshape Mount Grassy
Point   Stanley

4
                      Seal Point

Fitzmaurice
Bay
Surprise   Seal
Bay   Bay

                Stokes
                Point

Rocky
Cape
Beach
rayfish
Creek
Hellyer
Rocky Cape
Sisters   Sisters
Hills   Beach
Montumana   Boat Harbour
A2   Table Cape
        Flowerdale
Myalla   Wynyard
        Lapoinya   Seabrook   Doctors Rocks
Milabena   Camdale
Meunna   Calder Oldina   Somerset   Burnie
Hills   Elliott   A10
Preolenna   Mount   Heybridge   Sulphur Creek
antom   Pruarra Myrtle   Stowport   Penguin
Peak   Hill   Yolla South Elliott West   Turners Point
                                       Pine   Beach   Sorell
        Henrietta   Cuprona   Leith Hawley Beach
Hyena   Ridgley   Natone   1   Shearwater
Hill   Takone   Camena   Ferndene Ulverstone
        West   Riana Mount Gawler Forth Don Devonport Wesley Vale
Taylors Takone   Riana   Moriarty
Hill   Tewkesbury Highclere Upper   North Abbotsham Quoiba Spreyton Latrobe
        Oonah   Natone Motton   Kindred Melrose
                        Hampshire   South   Mount   Spalford Paloona Bonneys
Hellyer   Riana Lorymer Sprent   Tier Sassafras
Gorge   Lower
Parrawe HELLYER   Preston   Barrington
        GORGE   Mount   Heka   Lower
SAVAGE STATE   Housetop   Warringa   Wilmot Barrington Railton
RIVER   RESERVE Companion   Upper   Nook Merseylea
IONAL   Hill   Loongana Castra   Sheffield Stoodley
PARK   Belmont Saint   Range Nietta   Wilmot West   Kimberley
Magnet Range Hill Valentines   Kentish
        Gatcomb Peak   Mount   Narrawa   Roland Paradise Beulah
Mount   Plain   Everett South Nietta   Promised Land   Lower Weegena
Bischoff   Guildford Mount   Black   Erriba Staverton Gowrie Park Beulah
Mount   Two Tor   Bluff   Moina Cethana   Mount Dunorlan
Cleveland   Hummocks Mount   BLACK BLUFF   Vandyke Magog
Waratah   Mount   Cattley NATURE   Gowrie Park
        Mount   Moory   RECREATION Stormont Mount   Gog Range
B23   Pearse Mount   AREA   Claude   Mole
                Prospect   Lorinna   Liena   Creek Chudleigh
RIDGE   Mountain   Daisy   Mayberry
EGIONAL Netherby   Dell   Marakoopa Caveside
RESERVE Plain   Middlesex Emu   Cave
Mount   Mount   Plains Plains
Ramsay   Cripps

G   H   I   J   K   L

TOURING MAPS

Camping GUIDE TO TASMANIA | MAP 2

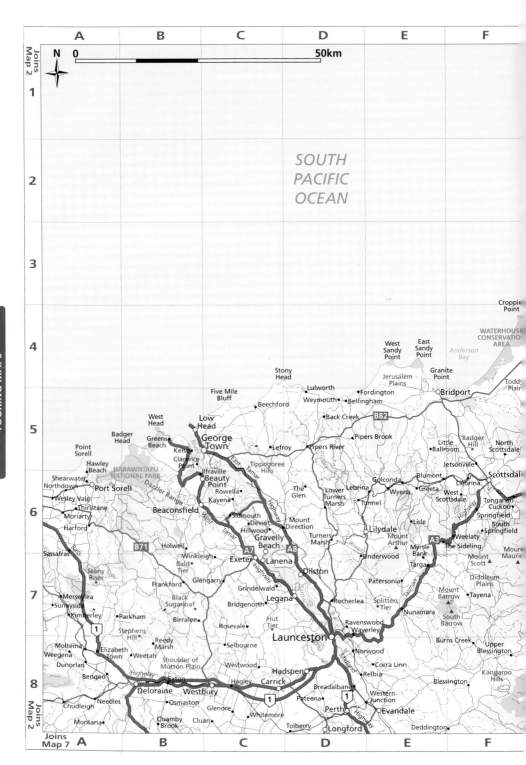

N   0   50km

SOUTH
PACIFIC
OCEAN

Croppie
Point

WATERHOUSE
CONSERVATIO
AREA

West
Sandy
Point

East
Sandy
Point

Anderson
Bay

Stony
Head

Jerusalem
Plains

Granite
Point

Todd
Plain

Five Mile
Bluff

Lulworth

Fordington

Bridport

Beechford

Weymouth
Bellingham

West
Head

Low
Head

Back Creek

B82

Badger
Head

Greens
Beach

George
Town

Lefroy

Pipers River

Pipers Brook

Little
Ballroom

Badger
Hill

North
Scottsdale

Point
Sorell

Kelso

Clarence
Point

Tippogoree
Hills

Jetsonville

Hawley
Beach

NARAWNTAPU
NATIONAL PARK

Ilfraville
Beauty
Point

The
Glen

Lower
Turners
Marsh

Lebrina

Golconda

Blumont

Lietinna

Scottsdal

Shearwater
Northdown

Port Sorell

Dazzler Range

Rowella

Wyena

Greeta

West
Scottsdale

Tonganah
Cuckoo

Wesley Vale
Thirlstane

Kayena

Tunnel

Lisle

Springfield

Moriarty

Beaconsfield

Sidmouth

Mount
Direction

South
Springfield

Harford

Deviot

Hillwood

Lilydale

Mount
Arthur

Weelaty

Sassafras

Holwell

Winkleigh
Bald
Tier

Gravelly
Beach

Turners
Marsh

Myrtle
Bank

The Sideling

Moun
Mauric

B71

A7

Exeter

Lanena

A8

Dilston

Underwood

Targa

A3

Mount
Scott

Stony
Rises

Frankford

Glengarry

Patersonia

Diddleum
Plains

Merseylea

Black
Sugarloaf

Grindelwald

Legana

Rocherlea

Splitters
Tier

Mount
Barrow

Tayena

Sunnyside
Kimberley

Parkham

Birralee

Bridgenorth

Nunamara

South
Barrow

Stephens
Hill

Rosevale

Hut
Tier

Ravenswood
Waverley

Burns Creek

Upper
Blessington

Moltema
Weegena

Elizabeth
Town

Reedy
Marsh

Selbourne

Launceston

Norwood

Dunorlan

Weetah

Shoulder of
Mutton Plain

Westwood

Corra Linn

Kangaroo
Hills

Bengeo

Highway

Eaton

Hagley

Hadspen

Relbia

Blessington

Deloraine

Westbury

Carrick

Breadalbane

Western
Junction

Chudleigh

Needles

Osmaston

Glenore

Whitemore

Pateena

Perth

Evandale

Montana

Quamby
Brook

Cluan

Toiberry

Longford

Deddington

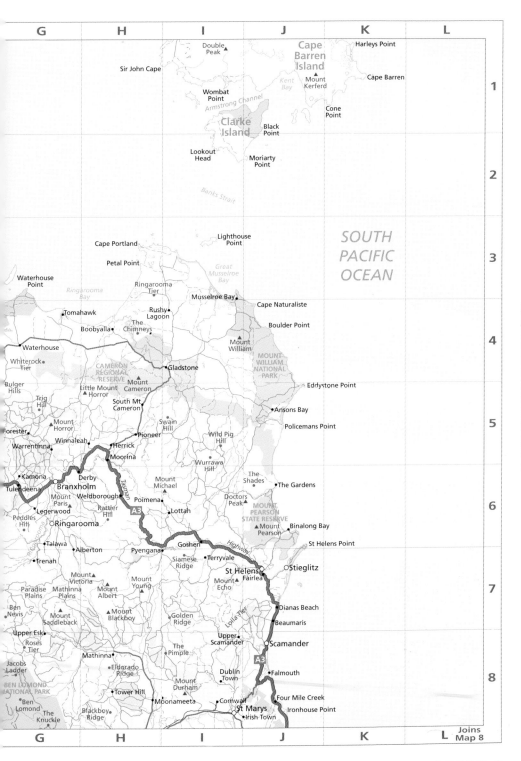

Double Peak
Sir John Cape
Cape Barren Island
Harleys Point
Mount Kerferd
Cape Barren
Kent Bay
Wombat Point
Armstrong Channel
Cone Point
Clarke Island
Black Point
Lookout Head
Moriarty Point

1

Banks Strait

2

Lighthouse Point
SOUTH PACIFIC OCEAN
Cape Portland
Petal Point
Great Musselroe Bay

3

Waterhouse Point
Ringarooma Bay
Ringarooma Tier
Musselroe Bay
Cape Naturaliste
Tomahawk
Rushy Lagoon
Boulder Point
Boobyalla
The Chimneys
Mount William
Waterhouse
MOUNT WILLIAM NATIONAL PARK

4

Whiterock Tier
CAMERON REGIONAL RESERVE
Mount Cameron
Bulger Hills
Little Mount Horror
Eddystone Point
Trig Hill
South Mt Cameron
Forester
Mount Horror
Swain Hill
Winnaleah
Pioneer
Wild Pig Hill
Arsons Bay
Warrentinna
Herrick
Policemans Point

5

Moorina
Wurrawa Hill
Kamona
Derby
Mount Michael
The Shades
The Gardens
Tulendeena
Branxholm
Tasman
Doctors Peak
Mount Paris
Weldborough
Poimena
MOUNT PEARSON STATE RESERVE
Legerwood
Rattler Hill
A3
Lottah
Mount Pearson
Binalong Bay
Peddles Hill
Ringarooma
St Helens Point

6

Talawa
Alberton
Pyengana
Goshen
Highway
Trenah
Siamese Ridge
Terryvale
Mount Victoria
St Helens
Stieglitz
Mount Young
Mount Echo
Fairlea
Paradise Plains
Mathinna Plains
Mount Albert

7

Ben Nevis
Mount Saddleback
Mount Blackboy
Golden Ridge
Dianas Beach
Upper Esk
Roses Tier
Lolla Tier
Beaumaris
Mathinna
The Pimple
Upper Scamander
Scamander
Jacobs Ladder
Eldorado Ridge
Dublin Town
Falmouth
BEN LOMOND NATIONAL PARK
Mount Durham
A3

8

Ben Lomond
Tower Hill
Moonameeta
Cornwall
Four Mile Creek
The Knuckle
Blackboy Ridge
St Marys
Ironhouse Point
Irish Town

Joins Map 8

TOURING MAPS

	A	B	C	D	E	F

1

Mount Sunday ▲

Badger Plains •

Savage River •

ARTHUR-PIEMAN CONSERVATION AREA

West Plain

• Longback

Moun Meredith ▲

MEREDITH RANGE REGIONA RESERVE

Mount Donaldson ▲

Meredith Range

Rupert Point •

Piemar

• Corinna

Mount Livingstone ▲

Mount Lindsay ▲

Pieman Head •

Conical Rocks Point •

Yarrana Hill •

Bernafai Ridge •

2

Ahrberg Bay

• Reece Dam

River

Wester Hills

Granville Harbour •

Mount Heemskirk ▲

3

MOUNT HEEMSKIRK REGIONAL RESERVE

Mount Agnew ▲

Zeehan •

Austral •

Trial Harbour •

Moun Zeeha ▲

B27

4

Henty • Dunes

Ocean Beach

5

Strahan •

Regatta Point •

SOUTHERN OCEAN

Hells Gates

Macquarie Heads •

Kelly Channel

6

Sloop Point •

Gorge Point •

Birthday Bay

7

Varna Bay

Hibbs Bay

8

Point Hibbs •

Spero Bay

N

0

50km

A	B	C	D	E	F

MAP 5 | Camping GUIDE TO TASMANIA

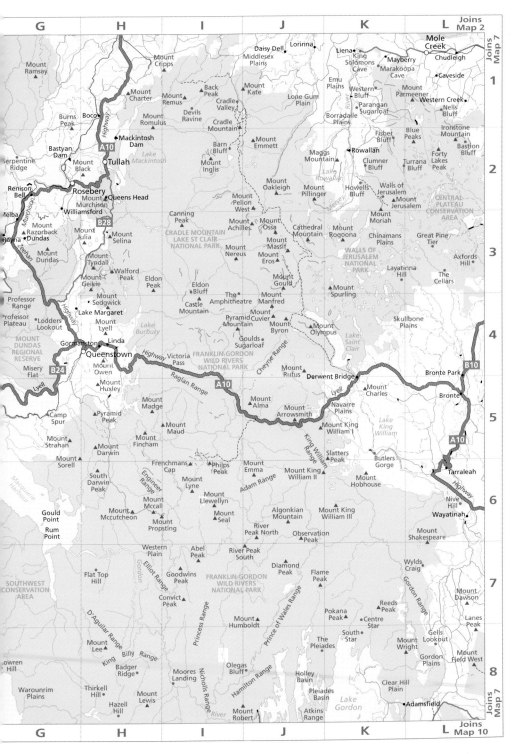

1

Mole
Creek

Daisy Dell   Lorinna
Middlesex   Liena   Chudleigh
Plains   King   Mayberry
Solomons   Marakoopa   Caveside
Mount   Cave   Cave
Cripps   Emu   Western   Mount
Plains   Bluff   Parmeener
Mount   Western Creek
Charter   Mount   Mount   Kate   Lone Gum   Parangan   Western Creek
Remus   Back   Plain   Sugarloaf   Nells
Mount   Peak   Borradaile   Bluff
Romulus   Devils   Cradle   Plains   Fisher   Ironstone
Ravine   Valley   Bluff   Blue   Mountain
Boco   Cradle   Maggs   Peaks
Burns   Mountain   Mount   Mountain   Bastion
Peak   Mount   Emmett   Clumner   Turrana   Forty   Bluff
Black   Barn   Mount   Bluff   Bluff   Lakes
Bluff   Mount   Inglis   Rowallan   Peak
Mackintosh   Rowallan   Howells
Dam   Mount   Bluff   Walls of
Bastyan   Mount   Oakleigh   Mount   Jerusalem
Dam   Tullah   Mount   Pillinger   Mount   CENTRAL
Serpentine   Murchison   Pelion   Jerusalem   PLATEAU
Ridge   Roseberry   West   Mount   CONSERVATION
Renison   Mount   Queens Head   Canning   Moriah   AREA
Bell   Williamsford   Peak   Mount   Mount
Melba   Murchison   Achilles   Ossa   WALLS OF
Mount   B28   Cathedral   Mount   JERUSALEM
Razorback   Mount   Mount   Mountain   Rogoona   Chinamans   Great Pine
Ravna   Dundas   Julia   Selina   CRADLE MOUNTAIN   Plains   Tier
Zeehan   LAKE ST CLAIR   Mount   Layatinna
Mount   NATIONAL PARK   Mount   Massif   Nereus   Mount   Hill   The
Dundas   Mount   Spurling   Cellars
Tyndall   Mount   Mount   WALLS OF   Axfords
Eros   Gould   JERUSALEM   Hill
Walford   NATIONAL
Professor   Peak   Eldon   Eldon   PARK
Range   Mount   Peak   Bluff   The   Mount
Geikie   Amphitheatre   Manfred   Skullbone
Professor   Castle   Mount   Plains
Plateau   Mount   Mountain   Cuvier   Mount
Sedgwick   Lake   Pyramid   Byron   Mount
Lodders   Lake Margaret   Burbury   Mountain   Goulds   Mount   Olympus   Lake
Lookout   Mount   Sugarloaf   Cheyne Range   Saint
Lyell   Linda   FRANKLIN-GORDON   Clair
MOUNT   Gormanston   Victoria   WILD RIVERS   Mount
DUNDAS   Queenstown   Pass   NATIONAL PARK   Rufus   Derwent Bridge   Bronte Park
REGIONAL   Mount   Highway   Mount   B10
RESERVE   Misery   Owen   Raglan Range   A10   Lyell   Charles
Flat   B24   Mount   Navarre   Bronte
Huxley   Mount   Plains
Lyell   Alma   Mount   Lake
Camp   Arrowsmith   Mount King   King
Spur   Pyramid   Mount   William I   William   A10
Peak   Madge   Slatters   Butlers
Mount   Mount   Peak   Gorge
Strahan   Mount   Maud   Mount   King   Tarraleah
Darwin   Mount   Frenchmans   Emma   William II   Mount
Mount   Fincham   Cap   Philps   Mount   Hobhouse   Nive
Sorell   South   Peak   Lyne   Adam Range   Hill
Marquarie   Darwin   Engineer   Mount   Wayatinah
Harbour   Peak   Range   Mount   Llewellyn   Algonkian   Mount King
Gould   Mccall   Mountain   William III   Mount
Point   Mount   Mount   Mount   Shakespeare
Rum   Mccutcheon   Propsting   Seal   River   Observation
Point   Peak North   Peak   Wylds
Western   Abel   River Peak   Craig
Plain   Peak   South   Diamond   Flame   Mount
Flat Top   Peak   Peak   Gordon Range   Dawson
SOUTHWEST   Hill   Goodwins   FRANKLIN-GORDON   Lanes
CONSERVATION   Peak   WILD RIVERS   Pokana   Reeds   Peak
AREA   Convict   NATIONAL PARK   Peak   Peak   Gells
Peak   Mount   Centre   Lookout
Mount   Humboldt   Star   Mount   Gordon
Lee   South   Wright   Field West
King   Billy   Range   The   Star   Plains
Pleiades   Olegas   Mount
Warounrim   Thirkell   Moores   Bluff   Holley   Clear Hill
Plains   Hill   Mount   Landing   Basin   Plain
Hazell   Lewis   Pleiades   Adamsfield
Hill   Mount   Basin   Atkins   Lake
Robert   Range   Gordon

TOURING MAPS

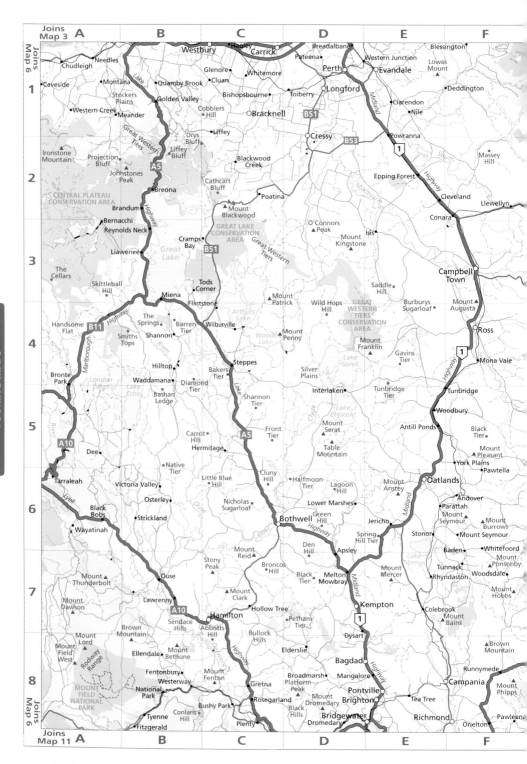

A   B   C   D   E   F

Chudleigh   Needles
Caveside   Montana   Quamby Brook   Glenore   Whitemore   Westbury   Hagley   Carrick   Breadalbane   Pateena   Western Junction   Blessington   Lowes Mount
Western Creek   Stockers Plains   Golden Valley   Cluan   Bishopsbourne   Toiberry   Perth   Evandale   Deddington
Meander   Cobblers Hill   Longford   Clarendon   Nile

1

Great Western Tiers   Drys Bluff   Liffey   Bracknell   B51   Powranna   1   Massey Hill
Ironstone Mountain   Projection Bluff   Liffey Bluff   Blackwood Creek   Cressy   B53
Johnstones Peak   Cathcart Bluff   Epping Forest   Highway   Cleveland

2

CENTRAL PLATEAU CONSERVATION AREA   Breona   Poatina   Llewellyn
Brandum   Mount Blackwood   O'Connors Peak   Isis   Conara
Bernacchi   GREAT LAKE CONSERVATION AREA   Mount Kingston
Reynolds Neck   Cramps Bay   B51   Great Western Tiers
Liawenee   Great Lake   Campbell Town

3

The Cellars   Skittleball Hill   Tods Corner   Saddle Hill   Burburys Sugarloaf   Mount Augusta
Miena   Flintstone   Mount Patrick   Wild Hops Hill   GREAT WESTERN TIERS CONSERVATION AREA   Ross
Handsome Flat   B11   The Springs   Barren Tier   Wilburville   Arthurs Lake   Mount Penny   Mount Franklin   Gavins Tier   Mona Vale
Shannon   Woods Lake   Lake Sorell

4

Bronte Park   Smiths Tops   Hilltop   Bakers Tier   Steppes   Silver Plains   Tunbridge Tier   Tunbridge
Waddamana   Diamond Tier   Shannon Tier   Interlaken   Woodbury
Dee   Bashan Ledge   Lake Echo   Lake Crescent   Mount Serat   Antill Ponds   Black Tier
Tarraleah   A10   Carrot Hill   Hermitage   A5   Front Tier   Table Mountain   Mount Pleasant   York Plains   Pawtella

5

Native Tier   Little Blue Hill   Cluny Hill   Halfmoon Tier   Lagoon Hill   Mount Anstey   Oatlands   Andover
Victoria Valley   Nicholas Sugarloaf   Lower Marshes   Parattah   Mount Seymour   Mount Burrows
Black Bobs   Osterley   Green Hill   Jericho   Stonor   Mount Seymour   Whiteford
Wayatinah   Strickland   Bothwell   Spring Hill Tier   Apsley   Baden   Mount Ponsonby

6

Mount Thunderbolt   Stony Peak   Den Hill   Apsley   Mount Mercer   Tunnack   Woodsdale
Mount Dawson   Lawrenny   Broncos Hill   Black Tier   Melton Mowbray   Rhyndaston   Mount Hobbs
Mount Clark   Hollow Tree   Kempton   Colebrook
Ouse   A10   Sendace Hills   Hamilton   Petham Tier   1   Mount Bains

7

Mount Lord   Brown Mountain   Abbotts Hill   Bullock Hills   Elderslie   Dysart   Brown Mountain
Mount Field West   Ellendale   Mount Bethune   Broadmarsh   Mangalore   Bagdad   Runnymede
Rodway Range   Fentonbury   Mount Fenton   Gretna   Platform Peak   Mount Dromedary   Campania   Mount Phipps
MOUNT FIELD NATIONAL PARK   Westerway   National Park   Rosegarland   Black Hills   Pontville   Brighton   Tea Tree
Tyenne   Conlans Hill   Bushy Park   Plenty   Dromedary   Bridgewater   Richmond   Orielton   Pawleena
Fitzgerald

8

TOURING MAPS

MAP 7 | Camping GUIDE TO TASMANIA

G   H   I   J   K   L

1

2

3

4

5

6

7

8

Tower
Hill

Blackboy
Ridge

Mangana

Dublin Town
Mount
Nicholas
Cornwall

Four Mile Creek
Ironhouse Point

Mount
Durham

St Marys

Break O'Day
Plains   Gray
Bare   Gray
Rock   Hills

Mount
Elephant   Wardlaws Point

Ben
Lomond

BEN LOMOND
NATIONAL PARK

atmans
ookout   Storys
Creek   Sawpit
Ridge   Mount
Clara   Fingal

Rossarden

CASTLE
CARY
REGIONAL
RESERVE

Dogwood
Hill   Chain of Lagoons
Piccaninny Point

A4   Mount
Edgecombe   Mount
Malcolm

Fingal
Tier

Mount
ount   Castle
hristie   Cary   St Pauls
Dome   Mount
Foster   Mount
Puzzler   Mount
Punter   Lookout
Hill

A3
Seymour

ount   Avoca   Mount
St Peter   Mount
Slaughter   Mount
St John   DOUGLAS-APSLEY
NATIONAL PARK
Douglas River

Royal
George   Pennefathers
Knob   Mount
Allen

Esk   Mount
Henry   Mount
Andrew

Campbell
Town
Mountain   Lewis
Hill   Lynes
Sugarloaf   Bicheno

ose
rae   Snow
Hill   Tar
Hill   Cape Lodi

Teatree
Hill   Ferrars
Tier   Butlers Point

B34   Island
Hill   Lake
Leake   Cranbrook   Rogers
Hill

apling
Hill   Mount
Morriston   Eagle
Ridge   Moulting
Lagoon   Mount
Peter

Mount
Paul   Friendly Point

FREYCINET
NATIONAL
PARK

Little Blue
Tier   A3   Swansea   Coles Bay   Cape Tourville

Burburys
Tier   Gentle
Annie   Mount
Dove

Skippys
Tier   Webber
Point   Great
Oyster
Bay   Cape Forestier

Stoneyard
Hill   Mount
Tooms   Shelly Point   Mount
Freycinet

Dowlings
Sugarloaf   Weatherhead
Point   Freycinet
Peninsula

Green
Tier   Mount
Lofty   Cape Degerando

emont   Boags Point   Schouten Passage

Marshalls
Tier   Royalty
Ridge   Little
Swanport   Seaford Point   Schouten
Island   Cape Sonnerat

Cape Faure

Ravensdale   Point Bailly

Mount
Murray   SOUTH
PACIFIC
OCEAN

Mount
Douglas   Triabunna   Cape
Bougainville

Louisville

Buckland   A3   Orford   Cape
Boullanger

Spring
Beach   Darlington

Mount
Calvary   Loafers
Hill   Rheban   Mount
Maria

Mount
Morrison   MARIA ISLAND
NATIONAL PARK   Mistaken Cape

Little Raggedy Head

Nugent   N

Mount
Walter   Cape
Peron   0   50km

G   H   I   J   K   L

TOURING MAPS

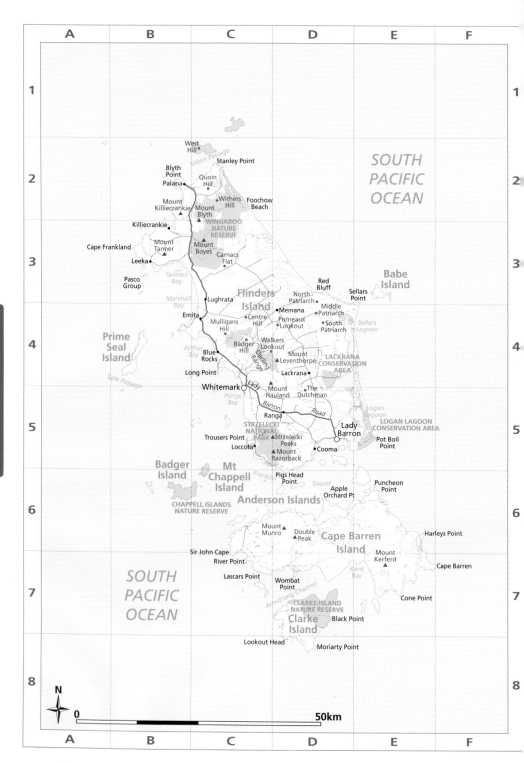

SOUTH
PACIFIC
OCEAN

West
Hill
Sisters Passage
Stanley Point

Blyth
Point
Palana
Quoin
Hill

Mount
Killiecrankie
Mount
Blyth
Withers
Hill
Foochow
Beach

Killiecrankie
WINGAROO
NATURE
RESERVE

Cape Frankland
Mount
Tanner
Mount
Boyes
Carnacs
Flat

Leeka
Babe
Island

Pasco
Group
Tanners
Bay
Red
Bluff
Sellars
Point

Marshall
Bay
Lughrata
Flinders
Island
North
Patriarch
Middle
Patriarch
Sellars
Lagoon

Emita
Memana
Furneaux
Lookout
South
Patriarch

Prime
Seal
Island
Mulligans
Hill
Centre
Hill

Arthur
Bay
Walkers
Lookout

Blue
Rocks
Badger
Hill
Mount
Leventhorpe
LACKRANA
CONSERVATION
AREA

Long Point
Darling
Range
Lackrana

Safe Passage
Whitemark
Lady
Mount
Hauland
The
Dutchman
Logan
Lagoon

Parrys
Bay
Barron
Road
LOGAN LAGOON
CONSERVATION
AREA

Ranga
Lady
Barron

STRZELECKI
NATIONAL
PARK
Strzelecki
Peaks
Cooma
Pot Boil
Point

Trousers Point
Loccota
Mount
Razorback

Badger
Island
Mt
Chappell
Island
Franklin
Pigs Head
Point

Anderson Islands
Sound
Apple
Orchard Pt
Puncheon
Point

CHAPPELL ISLANDS
NATURE RESERVE

Mount
Munro
Double
Peak
Cape Barren
Island
Harleys Point

SOUTH
PACIFIC
OCEAN
Sir John Cape
River Point
Mount
Kerferd
Cape Barren

Lascars Point
Kent
Bay
Cone Point

Wombat
Point
Armstrong Channel
CLARKE ISLAND
NATURE RESERVE
Black Point

Clarke
Island

Lookout Head
Moriarty Point

N
0
50km

MAP 9 | Camping GUIDE TO TASMANIA

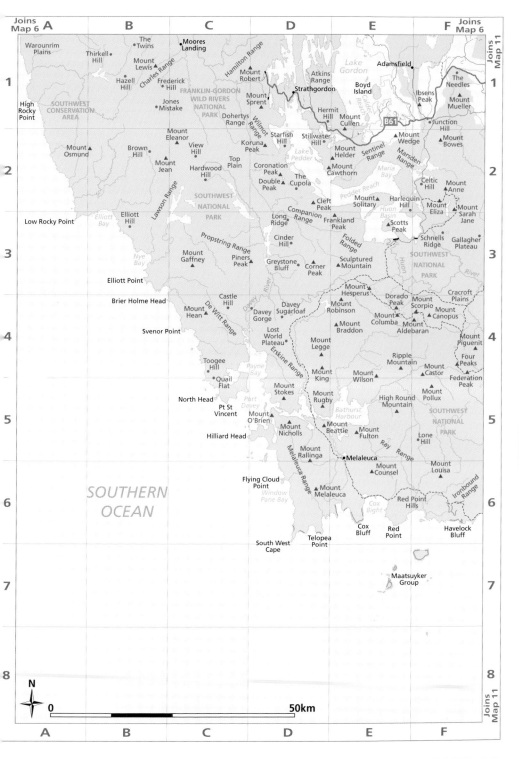

Joins
Map 6

Joins
Map 6

Joins
Map 11

A   B   C   D   E   F

1

Warounrim
Plains

The
Twins

Moores
Landing

Thirkell
Hill

Mount
Lewis

Charles Range

Frederick
Hill

Hamilton Range

Mount
Robert

Atkins
Range

Adamsfield

The
Needles

Hazell
Hill

FRANKLIN-GORDON
WILD RIVERS
NATIONAL
PARK

Strathgordon

Boyd
Island

Ibsens
Peak

High
Rocky
Point

SOUTHWEST
CONSERVATION
AREA

Jones
Mistake

Mount
Sprent

Dohertys
Range

Hermit
Hill

Mount
Cullen

Mount
Mueller

Junction
Hill

Wilmot Range

B61

2

Mount
Eleanor

View
Hill

Koruna
Peak

Starfish
Hill

Stillwater
Hill

Mount
Wedge

Mount
Bowes

Mount
Osmund

Brown
Hill

Mount
Jean

Hardwood
Hill

Top
Plain

Lake
Pedder

Mount
Helder

Sentinel
Range

Marsden
Range

Celtic
Hill

Mount
Anne

Coronation
Peak

The
Cupola

Maria
Bay

Lawson Range

Double
Peak

Mount
Cawthorn

Pedder Reach

Huon

SOUTHWEST
NATIONAL
PARK

Cleft
Peak

Mount
Solitary

Harlequin
Hill

Mount
Eliza

Mount
Sarah
Jane

Companion
Range

Frankland
Peak

Huon
Basin

Elliott
Bay

Elliott
Hill

Long
Ridge

Scotts
Peak

3

Low Rocky Point

Propstring Range

Cinder
Hill

Folded
Range

Schnells
Ridge

Gallagher
Plateau

Nye
Bay

Mount
Gaffney

Piners
Peak

Greystone
Bluff

Corner
Peak

Sculptured
Mountain

SOUTHWEST
NATIONAL
PARK

Huon

River

Elliott Point

Dewey River

Mount
Hesperus

Dorado
Peak

Cracroft
Plains

4

Brier Holme Head

Castle
Hill

Davey
Sugarloaf

Mount
Robinson

Mount
Scorpio

Mount
Canopus

Mount
Hean

De Witt Range

Davey
Gorge

Mount
Columba

Mount
Aldebaran

Svenor Point

Lost
World
Plateau

Mount
Braddon

Mount
Piguenit

Mount
Legge

Ripple
Mountain

Four
Peaks

Erskine Range

Payne
Bay

Toogee
Hill

Quail
Flat

Mount
King

Mount
Wilson

Mount
Castor

Federation
Peak

North Head

Pt St
Vincent

Port
Davey

Mount
Stokes

Mount
Rugby

High Round
Mountain

Mount
Pollux

5

Mount
O'Brien

Bathurst
Harbour

SOUTHWEST
NATIONAL
PARK

Hilliard Head

Mount
Nicholls

Mount
Beattie

Mount
Fulton

Lone
Hill

Ray Range

Mount
Rallinga

Mount
Louisa

Melaleuca

Mount
Counsel

Melaleuca Range

6

Flying Cloud
Point

Window
Pane Bay

Mount
Melaleuca

Cox
Bight

Red Point
Hills

Ironbound Range

SOUTHERN
OCEAN

Cox
Bluff

Red
Point

Havelock
Bluff

South West
Cape

Telopea
Point

7

Maatsuyker
Group

8

N

0   50km

A   B   C   D   E   F

TOURING MAPS

Camping GUIDE TO TASMANIA | **MAP 10**

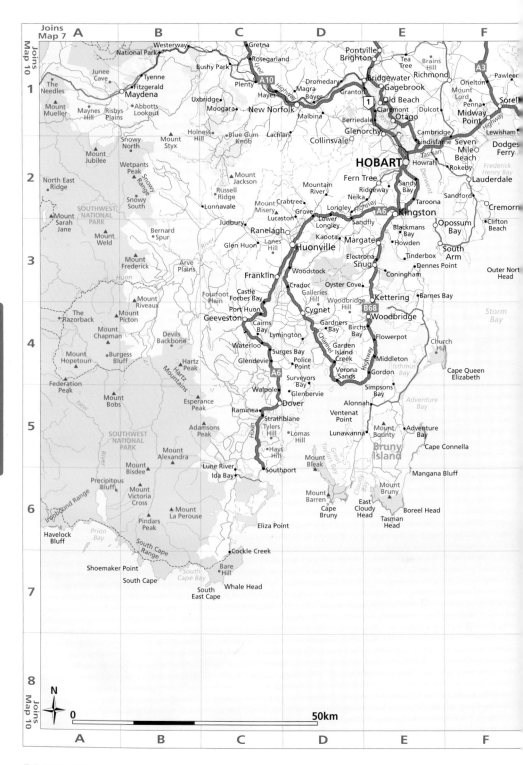

	A	B	C	D	E	F

1

Westerway
National Park
Junee
Cave
Tyenne
The
Needles
Fitzgerald
Mount
Mueller
Maydena
Maynes
Hill
Risbys
Plains
Abbotts
Lookout
Bushy Park
Plenty
A10
Uxbridge
Moogara
Hayes
New Norfolk
Gretna
Rosegarland
Dromedary
Magra
Boyer
Granton
Malbina
Berriedale
Pontville
Brighton
Bridgewater
Gagebrook
Old Beach
Claremont
Otago
Glenorchy
Tea
Tree
Brains
Hill
Richmond
Orielton
Mount
Lord
Dulcot
Cambridge
Lindisfarne
A3
Pawleer
Penna
Midway
Point
Sorell
Lewisham
Dodges
Ferry

2

North East
Ridge
Mount
Jubilee
Snowy
North
Mount
Styx
Wetpants
Peak
Snowy
Range
Russell
Ridge
Snowy
South
SOUTHWEST
NATIONAL
PARK
Holness
Hill
Lonnavale
Blue Gum
Knob
Lachlan
Mount
Jackson
Collinsvale
Mountain
River
Crabtree
Mount
Misery
Grove
Fern Tree
Ridgeway
Neika
HOBART
Howrah
Sandy
Bay
Taroona
Seven
Mile
Beach
Rokeby
Frederick
Henry Bay
Lauderdale
Sandford
Cremorn

3

Mount
Sarah
Jane
Mount
Weld
Mount
Frederick
Bernard
Spur
Arve
Plains
Judbury
Glen Huon
Ranelagh
Lanes
Hill
Huonville
Lower
Longley
Longley
Kaoota
Sandfly
Margate
A6
Kingston
Blackmans
Bay
Howden
Tinderbox
Opossum
Bay
South
Arm
Dennes Point
Clifton
Beach
Outer Nort
Head

4

The
Razorback
Mount
Riveaux
Mount
Picton
Mount
Chapman
Devils
Backbone
Hartz
Peak
Hartz
Mountains
Fourfoot
Plain
Castle
Forbes Bay
Port Huon
Geeveston
Cairns
Bay
Waterloo
Glendevie
Franklin
Cradoc
Woodstock
Galleries
Hill
Oyster Cove
Woodbridge
Hill
Cygnet
Lymington
Surges Bay
Police
Point
A6
Gardners
Bay
Birchs
Bay
Garden
Island
Creek
Channel
Verona
Sands
B68
Woodbridge
Kettering
Barnes Bay
Flowerpot
Middleton
Gordon
Church
Hill
Cape Queen
Elizabeth
Storm
Bay

5

Mount
Hopetoun
Burgess
Bluff
Federation
Peak
Mount
Bobs
Esperance
Peak
Adamsons
Peak
Mount
Alexandra
Raminea
Walpole
Dover
Glenbervie
Strathblane
Tylers
Hill
Lomas
Hill
Surveyors
Bay
Simpsons
Bay
Alonnah
Ventenat
Point
Lunawanna
Mount
Bounty
Adventure
Bay
Cape Connella
Adventure
Bay
Bruny
Island
Green Taylors Bay
Isthmus
Bay

6

Ironbound Range
Havelock
Bluff
Prion
Bay
Mount
Bisdee
Precipitous
Bluff
Mount
Victoria
Cross
Pindars
Peak
Mount
La Perouse
Lune River
Ida Bay
Hays
Hill
Southport
Mount
Bleak
Eliza Point
Mount
Barren
Cape
Bruny
Mount
Bruny
East
Cloudy
Head
Cloudy Bay
Tasman
Head
Boreel Head
Mangana Bluff

7

South Cape
Range
Shoemaker Point
South Cape
South
Cape Bay
Cockle Creek
Bare
Hill
Whale Head
South
East Cape

8

N

0   50km

MAP 11 | Camping GUIDE TO TASMANIA

TOURING MAPS

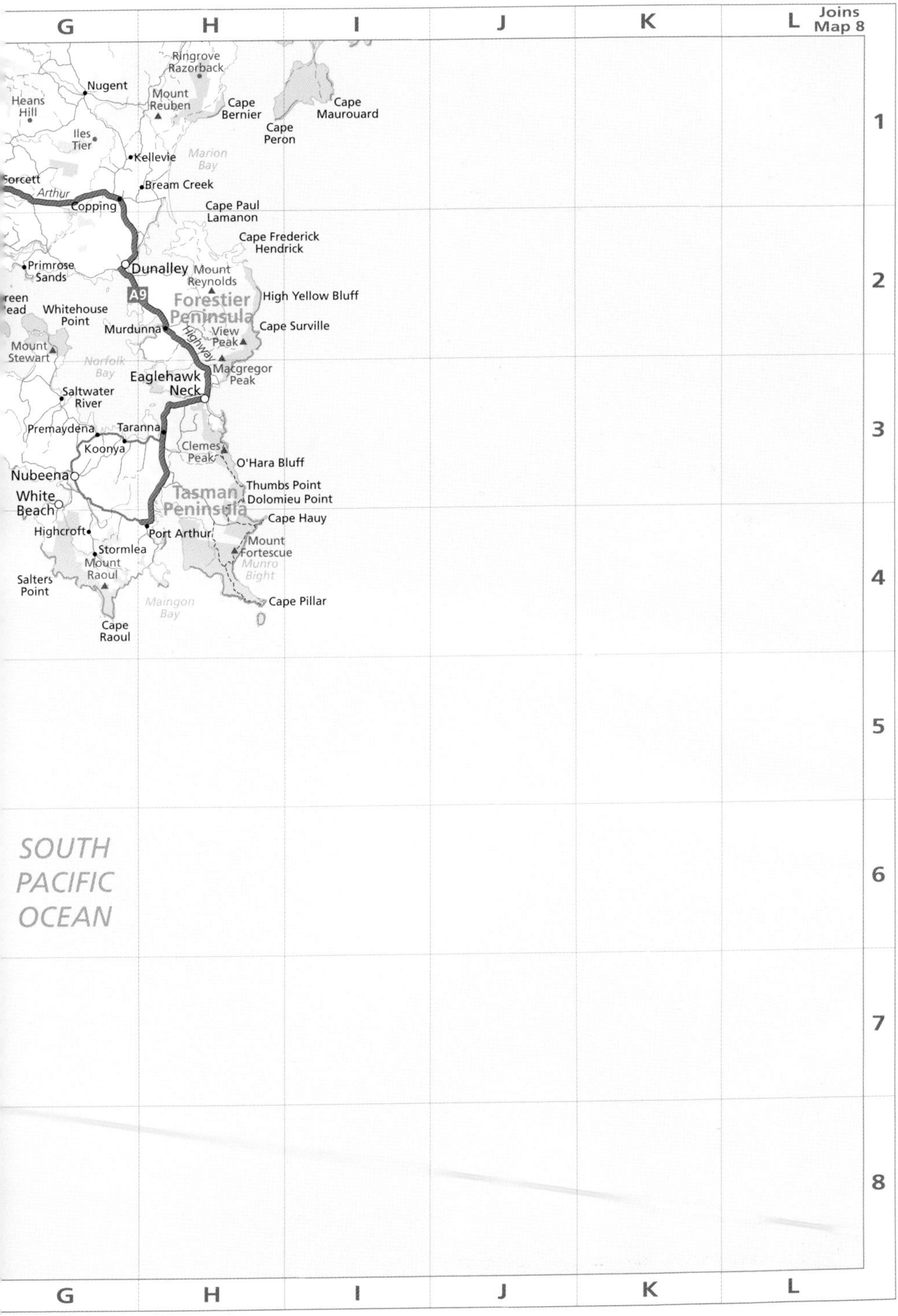

1

2

3

4

5

6

7

8

Ringrove Razorback
Nugent
Heans Hill
Mount Reuben
Cape Bernier
Cape Maurouard
Cape Peron
Iles Tier
Kellevie
Marion Bay
Sorcett
Arthur
Copping
Bream Creek
Cape Paul Lamanon
Cape Frederick Hendrick
Primrose Sands
Dunalley
Mount Reynolds
High Yellow Bluff
A9
Forestier Peninsula
reen ead
Whitehouse Point
Murdunna
View Peak
Cape Surville
Mount Stewart
Norfolk Bay
Macgregor Peak
Saltwater River
Eaglehawk Neck
Highway
Premaydena
Taranna
Koonya
Clemes Peak
O'Hara Bluff
Nubeena
Tasman Peninsula
Thumbs Point
Dolomieu Point
White Beach
Cape Hauy
Highcroft
Port Arthur
Mount Fortescue
Munro Bight
Stormlea
Salters Point
Mount Raoul
Maingon Bay
Cape Pillar
Cape Raoul

SOUTH PACIFIC OCEAN

Vehicle touring, South Arthur Forests

Parks, Forests, Reserves and Campsites Index

***Denotes areas with facilities (usually special
    access to toilets) for people
    with disabilities**

Lake St Clair — Lake St Clair Tourist Park

Campsite Index

* **Denotes areas with facilities (usually special access to toilets) for people with disabilities**

Lake Chisholm, South Arthur Forests

Boiling Billy and

Camping Guide to Tasmania is just one of a growing series of outdoor and souvenir guides from Boiling Billy and co-publishers Woodslane.

Boiling Billy have been publishing guides for the Australian outdoor enthusiast for nearly 17 years, and details of all their titles can be found at www.boilingbilly.net.au They are now co-publishing with Woodslane, one of Australia's leading book distributors and publishers. To browse through other titles available from Woodslane, visit www.woodslane.com.au If your local bookshop does not have stock of a Boiling Billy or Woodslane book, they can easily order it for you. In case of difficulty please contact our customer service team on 02 8445 2300 or order direct at www.boilingbilly.net.au.

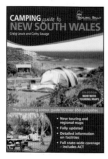

Camping Guide to NSW 5/e

$29.95

ISBN: 9781921203688

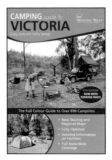

Camping Guide to Victoria 4/e

$29.95

ISBN: 9781921203671

Camping Guide to South Australia 3/e

$29.95

ISBN: 9781921203985

Camping Guide to Western Australia 3/e

$29.99

ISBN: 9781921606168

Camping Guide to Queensland 4/e

$29.99

ISBN: 9781921606151

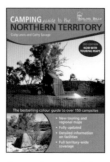

Camping Guide to the Northern Territory 3/e

$29.95

ISBN: 9781921203978

Robert Pepper's 4WD Handbook

$44.95

ISBN: 9781921874789

Australian Bush Cooking 3/e

$34.95

ISBN: 9781921203930